Arthur Evelyn Barnes-Lawrence

A Churchman to Churchmen

Arthur Evelyn Barnes-Lawrence

A Churchman to Churchmen

ISBN/EAN: 9783337367381

Printed in Europe, USA, Canada, Australia, Japan

Cover: Foto ©Paul-Georg Meister /pixelio.de

More available books at **www.hansebooks.com**

EIGHTH THOUSAND.

A CHURCHMAN

TO

CHURCHMEN.

*A SERIES OF LECTURES ON MATTERS OF
CONTROVERSY AT THE PRESENT DAY.*

BY

A. E. BARNES-LAWRENCE, M.A.,

*Late Exhibitioner of Worcester College, Oxford.
Vicar of St. Michael and All Angels, Blackheath Park, S.E.*

WITH PREFACE BY

H. C. G. MOULE, M.A.,

*Principal of Ridley Hall, and late Fellow of Trinity College,
Cambridge.*

" τῷ μὲν γὰρ ἀληθεῖ πάντα συνᾴδει τὰ ὑπάρχοντα."
"With the truth all facts and realities agree."
                                        ARISTOTLE.

𝔅𝔩𝔞𝔠𝔨𝔥𝔢𝔞𝔱𝔥:

HENRY BURNSIDE.

LONDON: SIMPKIN, MARSHALL & CO.

1894.

PREFACE.

THE responsibility of publishing these Lectures must rest with my Congregation rather than myself. Delivered in Lent, at a time of much pressure, they were wrung from me by a sense of their need. It is indisputable that a large number of the most spiritual, active, and intelligent members of the Church of England are slowly drifting from her Communion, and are merely held together where they can enjoy a simple ritual in worship and Scriptural teaching. The reason is not far to seek. On all sides they observe practices tolerated, and doctrines avowed, from which this country was purged at the Reformation, and which they have been hitherto accustomed to associate with the Church of Rome. A deep distrust of the Bishops, and, in many cases, of the position of their own Church, has, beyond question, taken possession of their inmost souls. What is the consequence? They withhold their money from Diocesan objects, while they give splendidly to societies in which they have confidence ; they are often forced to attend chapel because they have been driven out of their parish church; they even contemplate Disestablishment as a possible escape from a state of things which has become intolerable. These Lectures are an honest attempt to reassure such disheartened Churchmen of the real teaching of their own historic Church. They are not exhaustive, they do not pretend to original research, they are simply designed as a help to those who cannot study large and expensive works; and already I have had the gratification of hearing some say that they are better Churchmen than they thought they were.

I have purposely made free use of Hooker; for Hooker, a very few years ago, was a final court of appeal to most High Churchmen. I must express my indebtedness for several quotations to Mr. Odom's excellent little volume, "The Church of England," and to Canon Fausset's "Scripture and Prayer-Book in Harmony"—now, I regret to hear, out of print. For the first part of the Lecture on the Lord's Supper I owe much to a careful analysis of Vogan by my friend the Hon. and Rev. W. T. Rice; other debts are, I think, acknowledged in their place. These addresses were taken down by a shorthand-writer, and I have not cared to alter their direct and personal character.

In conclusion, I will merely say that, while I have spoken plainly and unhesitatingly, I have endeavoured to do so in the spirit of our Collect for Quinquagesima Sunday:—

"O Lord, who hast taught us that all our doings without charity are nothing worth;

send Thy Holy Ghost, and pour into our hearts that most excellent gift of charity, the very bond of peace and of all virtues, without which whosoever liveth is counted dead before Thee : Grant this for Thine only Son Jesus Christ's sake. Amen."

A. E. B-L.

BLACKHEATH,
Whitsuntide, 1893.

PREFACE TO THE SECOND EDITION.

I REJOICE in the publication of "A Churchman to Churchmen." The book is valuable for its own sake ; and then, as a sign of the times, full of encouragement to those who love the Church of England as she really is. It is excellent in itself. Within its modest compass lies a mass of facts, arranged, discussed, and illustrated with great accuracy and ability ; and the facts are, too many of them, just those which have been either dropped out of sight, or carefully put out of sight, of recent years in quarters supposed to be specially true to .the Church. I for one thank God for this restatement, equally careful and popular, temperate and distinct, of what the English Church *really* says and *really* does not say, about Church, Ministry, and Sacraments. Not one sentence violates Christian kindliness and fairness. But the writer has found out how, all the more effectually, to˙ speak unpopular truth, and to contrast it with popular error, so that his words will be remembered. I think highly of all the lectures, and not least of the last. It brings the whole discussion to a practical issue in a way most stirring and suggestive, and not a day too soon.

The work is, moreover, a hopeful sign of the times. It is one of the many noteworthy symptoms of the right sort of Protestant revival in the Church. It betokens a renewed attention to our great Reformed Theologians on the part of cultivated parochial clergymen of a generation still in its prime. It shows how much such men are growingly alive to the impossibility of neglecting the distinctive doctrinal information of their people ; and then it puts all this in living contact with the question of personal conversion to God, personal consecration of self to His service, and personal holiness and righteousness of life in Christ.

May the Lord of the Word and of the Church bless the message of this book.

H. C. G. MOULE.

CAMBRIDGE,
June 24, 1893.

CONTENTS.

"The house of God, which is the Church of the living God."—I TIM. iii. 15.

THE Church—What is it? The question is absolutely important, but by no means new. It is a question that has been discussed through all the centuries of Christian faith. As early as the Epistles of Clement and Ignatius we hear of it; in the time of Cyprian it is a matter of fierce conflict; it is in debate in the time of Augustine; it continues to be so right down to the Reformation; it is hotly discussed still. Nor need we wonder; it is a right instinct which has made this topic a battle-field. This is no mere academic question, some matter for schoolmen only and theologians, rather it is one that touches all that is most vital to our soul's welfare, it affects our very salvation; and that is why I have without hesitation put it first in the list of subjects for Sunday evening consideration. All controversy is distasteful to me, nor need these matters be approached in a controversial spirit, but I have a duty to you as my people in a day of perplexity, and my object is rather to defend what is true, than to attack what is false.

I. The word "Church" is used in several different senses, but the main question to-day lies between two perfectly simple issues. Is "the Church" a spiritual and mystical body, invisible as a whole to man but visible to God ; or is it, to quote Mr. Sadler, who speaks, remember, for the High Church party, "always an outward and visible body, known by certain outward and visible marks"? Is it true that, "If our Services are to be Scriptural, they must give no countenance to the idea that there are two Churches—a visible and an invisible—to the former of which we are supposed to be admitted at our Baptism, while God has restricted saving grace to the latter. Our Services recognise but one Church, the visible, into which the person is admitted at Baptism" ("Church Doctrine," pp. 41, 85).

Where shall we look for guidance ? By a true instinct we turn at once to the New Testament, and confining ourselves for the moment to one of the Pauline Epistles, we find three wonderful figures of the Church. It is the Body of Christ. "He is Head over all things to the Church, which is His body, the fulness of Him that filleth all in all" (Eph. i. 22, 23). I have so recently dwelt upon this sublime theme, that I will but mention it now ; but whatever modern science has told us of the marvellous interdependence of the Head and the Members, such, at least spiritually, is that of Christ and His Church. Through the eyes of this Body He looks forth upon a world of dying men ; through its lips He asks the hopeless sinner, " Wilt thou be made whole ? " Through its hands He ministers bread to hungry souls ; on its feet He fain would go to " the uttermost parts of the earth," and claim what He has purchased for His own. The Church is the Fulfilment on earth of Divine grace.

Again, the Church is His glorious House (ii. 19–22), a Temple of which " each several building fitly joined together," growing in compactness, growing in extension (both thoughts are in the Greek), becomes an holy Sanctuary for the Lord Himself. His indwelling in His people is a blessed reality now, it is the pledge of still brighter reality hereafter. Yet again, the Church is the Bride of Christ. The sacred union of Holy Marriage, instituted in the world's opening glow, is what it is, that it may set forth the mystery of the Union of Christ and His Redeemed ; the Apostle says, " the twain become one flesh ; this mystery is great : but I speak in regard of Christ and of the Church " (v. 31, 32, R.V.).

And now, passing from the inspired words of the servant, listen reverently to the words of the Master. More wonderful than the figures of the Epistle is the simile of the life-union of " The Vine and the Branches " in the Gospel (John xv. 1–6), and surely most wonderful of all, the setting forth of that in-effable Oneness in the prayer of our great High Priest, " that they all may be one ; as Thou

Father, art in Me, and I in Thee, that they also may be one in Us" (John xvii. 21).

Is there one here who is not intuitively and immediately conscious that these passages describe a Union that is something more than the eyes of the world can see? But if the ties that link its members to Christ are mystical, spiritual, and invisible, it follows that the Church itself is also mystical, spiritual, and invisible, " The House of God which is the Church of the living God." And Luther's words are true, " That there is one Church, Holy, Catholic, and Apostolic, is an article of faith and not of sight."

Equally clear is the witness of the most eminent Churchmen to this momentous fact. No name stands higher than that of Hooker, and what does Hooker say? "For lack of diligent observation the difference, first between the Church of God mystical and visible, then between the visible, sound and corrupted, the oversights are neither few nor light that have been committed." I might quote from Jeremy Taylor, Isaac Barrow and many another, but let me give you the words of a more modern theologian, Dr. Chris. Wordsworth, the late eminent bishop, himself a High Churchman : "The Church is visible as far only as is seen by men ; it is invisible as it is known by God. The *visible* Church contains both good and bad ; the invisible consists of good only. In the visible are wheat and chaff, wheat and tares mixed together ; in the invisible, wheat alone. The one is the Church of the *called,* the other of the *elect of God only*" ("Theophilus Anglicanus," cd. ix. p. 14). It must be so :—

> " For She on Earth hath union
>   With God, the Three in One ;
> And mystic sweet communion,
>   With those whose rest is won.'

Our Church herself is equally outspoken. The Homily for Whit-Sunday defines the matter thus :—" The true Church is an universal congregation and fellowship of God's *faithful* and *elect* people, built upon the foundation of the apostles and prophets, Jesus Christ Himself being the head corner-stone." In her Ordinal she speaks of " Christ's sheep that are dispersed abroad, and His children who are in the midst of this naughty world." In her last Collect she exults in " the mystical body of Thy Son Jesus Christ, which is the blessed company of all faithful people." But it is in her 55th Canon that she dogmatically defines the Church thus :—" Ye shall pray for Christ's holy Catholic Church, that is, for the whole congregation of Christian people dispersed throughout the world, and especially for the Churches of England, Scotland,¹ and Ireland."

II. But in the New Testament the term " Church " is applied not only to the body mystical, but to separate communities of Christians ; and, mark this, it is just because men apply the attributes and graces of the

---

¹ Note that our Canon calls the *Presbyterian* Church of Scotland a *Church*.

Church of the Redeemed to one or another of these visible communities, that such fatal illusions are prevalent. It is important you should observe that no sooner had the infant church developed than we hear no longer of "the Church" but of "the churches." You recollect that St. Paul speaks of the "Churches of Galatia"; and even, where we should least expect it, of the "Churches of Judea"; and yet again, he writes, "The Churches of Christ salute you." Especially noteworthy it is that the ascended Lord Himself sends messages to "the seven Churches that are in Asia"; and in the wonderful close of the Book of Revelation He declares, "I, Jesus, have sent mine angel to testify unto you these things in the Churches." Surely this should make some pause; surely His language is in marked contrast to those reiterated words "the church," "the church," so loosely and vaguely used to-day. The Church as a single visible society on earth is not so addressed or spoken of by the Holy Ghost.

We cannot afford to be mistaken here. The spell of a false conception as to the Church has wrought untold misery on the earth, it has been one great spiritual instrument for enslaving the souls and even the bodies of men. In the third century Cyprian said, "There is no salvation outside the Church," meaning the visible community. The Romanist to-day says exactly the same, meaning the Roman Church; the High Churchman says, with wider charity but equal confusion, "Outside the Anglican,

Greek, and Roman communities, which together constitute The Church, there is no *security* of salvation." There always have been, and there always will be until the Chief Shepherd Himself is manifested, many "folds" of the one " flock." The effort, repeated again and again, to compel all Christ's sheep into *one* fold has always disastrously failed, and always must. Look back over the pages of history, and you will find that those that tell of such efforts are more deeply bloodstained than any other. Think of Simon de Montfort and the Albigenses ; of the Massacre of St. Bartholomew ; of the Revocation of the Edict of Nantes ; of Philip II., Alva, and the Netherlands ; of Mary and the Protestants ; of Elizabeth and the Romanists ;·of Laud and the Puritans ; of Charles II. and the Scottish Covenanters. Look around you, and think of the Stundists in Russia, of the Protestant congregations in Spain ; and, when you have summed up your observations, you will con-fess that the only visible results of such efforts are the martyrdom of some, the hypocrisy of others, the sullen resistance of many, and the undying hatred of all.

At the time of the Reformation the Roman Church exercised an overpowering influence ; she captivated the imagination as well as enslaved the conscience ; she exerted a vast temporal power ; resistance to her claims was sacrilege. In their struggle with the Re-formers, the Roman controversialists flung themselves on the antiquity, extent, and in-fluence of their Church. The reply was twofold. The Reformers acknowledged that Christ had left His promises to the Church, but denied that the Pope and Bishops were the Church so favoured ; rather was it an elect remnant, of which they themselves by grace were part. In other words, they revived the conception of the invisible Church of Christ. Their other reply, as I need not remind you, was to assert the true conditions of membership with Christ, and to declare that Justification was by faith only. By this New Testament doctrine alone, Christian souls, weak and isolated, dared to assert their independence of Rome, and to brave its thunders.

It was the secret of the Reformation. In her XIXth Article our Church affirms the Reformers' view :—

"The visible Church of Christ is a congregation of faithful men, in the which the pure Word of God is preached, and the Sacraments be duly ministered according to Christ's ordinance, in all those things that of necessity are requisite to the same. As the Church of Jerusalem, Alexandria, and Antioch, have erred ; so also the Church of Rome hath erred, not only in their living and manner of ceremonies, but also in matters of Faith."

The question which tortures thousands of souls to-day, which is the wailing keynote of Newman's *Apologia*, "In what Church is salvation to be found ?"[1] is based, says Dr. Wace, on essential error. If conscience bids

---

[1] See article " The Church " in *The Church and her Doctrine* (Nisbet), to which I am much indebted.

men change their church they are bound at their peril to do so, but the cardinal proposition of the Roman Church and of the modern Anglican, expressed by Mr. Gore, the latest spokesman of the Oxford school, in the following terms, " Membership in the true Church depends on membership in the visible Church on earth," is alike opposed to reason, to history, to the Prayer-Book, and to the New Testament.

III. Is, then, the right Organisation of the Church of Christ a matter of no importance? We cannot think so. Those solemn words, uttered at one of the most solemn moments of our Lord's life, "That they also may be one : as Thou, Father, art in Me, and I in Thee, that they also may be one in Us : that the world may believe that Thou hast sent Me," cannot be reconciled with our "unhappy divisions." Unity, visible unity, as the evidence of our Mission, a source of strength, and the fulfilment of the purpose of Christ, is what every Christian should work and pray for. Not but that even Unity can be bought too dear, when it is secured by the sacrifice of principle ; but Unity based on the three essential points of Christian Faith, Christian Life, and Christian Discipline, is for the glory of God.

It is as possessing these three notes that the Church of England claims to be a sound branch of the historic Catholic Church, and protests against the Roman Church as unsound, because she does not possess them. Our Church claims no perfection. " In the

2

visible Church, she insists, the evil is ever mingled with the good " (Art. XXVI.). You may remember the telling answer once given by a clergyman to one of his parishioners, who said she was about to leave the Church of her baptism, and join a perfect church. " Your purpose is excellent," he said, "and I hope you will succeed, only don't forget that so soon as you have joined such a church it will cease to be perfect." Our Church bitterly laments her shortcomings in the past, and blames herself for much of the nonconformity that exists ; but she has nevertheless the three cardinal points I just mentioned, and with these she links her historical claim.

Thus with regard to the Nonconformists her position is clear. She asserts in the first place *her Antiquity.* Some think she was a new Church at the Reformation in the six-teenth century. They are mistaken. Some think she was a new Church when Augustine landed in A.D. 596. They are mistaken. So early as the fourth century the British Church furnished martyrs in the terrible persecution under Diocletian ; and to one of them who refused to sacrifice to the gods, the familiar name of the church, town, and diocese of St. Albans is due. Earlier still, in the decree convening the Council of Nicea (A.D. 325) special mention is made of the Church of Britain. Earlier still, at the Council of Arles, in 314, we find her represented by the Bishops of York, London, and Caerleon ; and earlier still, Tertullian, a Roman writer, dating from A.D. 201, says : " Regions of the Britons, inaccessible to the Romans, have assuredly been subdued to Christ." [1]

All this proves the existence of our English Church more than three hundred years before the arrival of the Roman Mission under Augustine. At a time when Britain was parcelled out into many kingdoms there was only one Church, and, in view of some modern pretensions, I would have you remember that though we owe the see of Canterbury to Augustine, his mission was comparatively a failure in two respects. As a mission from the Pope it did not succeed. At that time the British Church had its own Liturgy, and sturdily refused Augustine's demands as to the time for observing Easter, as to the mode of baptism, and as to the tonsure. Its clergy, moreover, refused to be subject to the Pope. From the very first, therefore, centuries before

---

[1] The historian Gildas, who died at Glastonbury in A.D. 570, professes to give, as some think, a still earlier date to the British Church in the following words: " In the meantime, Christ the true Sun afforded his Rays, that is the knowledge of his Precepts to this Island, shivering with Icy-cold, and separate at a great distance from the visible Sun, not from the visible Firmament, but from the Supreme everlasting Power of Heaven. For we certainly know that in the latter end of the Reign of Tiberius that Sun appear'd to the whole World with his Glorious Beams, in which time his Religion was propagated without any impediment against the Will of the Roman Senate, death being threatened by that Prince to all who should inform against the Soldiers of Christ." But this passage, which writers have applied to the particular preaching of the gospel in Britain, seems rather to refer to the general liberty of preaching it throughout the Roman world. Stillingfleet says, " This I take to be Gildas his true meaning " (" Origines Britannicæ ").

the Council of Spires, our Church as regards Rome was a " Protestant " Church.

As a spiritual effort it also failed. Devotedly as Augustine worked in this part of the country, his converts too often lapsed into heathenism, as history shows ; and England as a whole was evangelised by other missionaries than those of the Roman Church. If you have ever read Bishop Lightfoot's " Leaders in the Northern Church," you will remember that not Augustine, but Columba and Aidan, were the true apostles of England. Iona, not Canterbury, became the light of Christendom. Not merely England and Scotland, but large tracts of the continent, were evangelised by the Irish missionaries, altogether apart from the influence and guidance of Rome. The Presbyter-Abbot of Iona, not the Pope, was their head ; and when there arose a question as to which they owed allegiance, they unhesitatingly chose the former. And it was due to him and his, under God, that this country ceased to be heathen, and accepted the name of Christ.

It cannot be too often repeated that for six hundred years England owed no allegiance to Rome, and that for the next thousand years there was always a strong national party protesting loudly against its usurpation, until it was finally shaken off. It is to their ancient Church, in the providence of God, that Englishmen, whether Churchmen or Nonconformists, mainly owe their Bible, their Christian liberty, their hopes of heaven. You have not forgotten how in A.D. 1213, when King

John sold his kingdom to the Pope and became his vassal, it was Stephen Langton, Archbishop of Canterbury, who headed the revolt of the Barons, and compelled the unworthy king to seal *Magna Charta*, that palladium of our national liberties ; nor how its first clause runs thus : "The Church of England shall be free, and hold her rights entire, and her liberties inviolate."

Once again, the Church of England asserts that she is a *National Church*, and she has good reason for doing so. It is not, remember, that she was ever established by Act of Parliament, for she existed centuries before Crown or Parliament did ; she was established not by legislative decree, but by evangelistic effort ; established, that is, privately in men's hearts long before she was publicly recognised by the State. All that the phrase, *by law established*, means, is that her Constitution, Liturgy, and Doctrine, drawn up by her own representatives, received the sanction of the State, and that the observance of them is enforceable by law. The case of the Nonconformists is exactly parallel : their Trust Deeds, drawn up by themselves, for the legal possession and succession of their own property and doctrine, would be of no authority whatever without the sanction of the State ; yet who would say that, because they availed themselves of such protection, the State gave them their property ? But you will readily perceive that the ancient Church of the country must be far more closely entwined with our whole legal fabric than any religious body of modern birth. I suppose that if Barnabas, instead of selling his land in Cyprus and giving the proceeds to the apostles, had legally conveyed it to the Church of Jerusalem, the title to it to-day would be more intricate than that of a freehold which has no particular history. So is it with the laws regulating the laws of the Church of England, compared with those regulating religious bodies outside her communion ;[1] and it is due to her ancient endowments held by immemorial title, which some to-day would seize for secular purposes, that she makes provision for the spiritual needs of multitudes for whom there is no other provision at all. Disestablishment means disendowment ; and disendowment means in hundreds of poor parishes the cessation of the present public means of grace. The chapel often cannot exist where the Church, owing to her endowments, can.[2] Speaking of disestablishment reminds me that our National Church secures three things. First, the public

[1] See "The Englishman's Brief on Behalf of his National Church " (S.P.C.K.).

[2] The following extract from a strong Liberationist paper suggests the advantages of endowments from another side : " A man with an income of £60 a year drawn from a few people whom he is bound to please cannot afford to speak his mind. We have observed such poor men painfully calculating the loss to their income if such and such persons were to take offence and leave the place. There are hundreds of Nonconformists who, laboriously treading out the corn, are muzzled and not unmuzzled. And this is our blessed voluntaryism, and for this we fight against (Church) endowments, and would have them devoted to relieving the rates for sewering and daving ! " (*The Christian World*).

acknowledgment by the State of the existence of God and of the work of Christ—no small matter, as a glance at France will tell you. " The union of Church and State," said Lord Eldon, " is not to make the Church political, but the State religious." Well did Dr. Owen, a Nonconformist, say to the Government of his day : " If it comes to this, that you say you have nothing to do with religion as rulers of the nation, God will quickly manifest that He hath nothing to do with you as rulers of the nation." Again, I say, look at France.

Second. A bulwark against the encroachments of Rome—as her past history might lead you to expect. Were our Church disestablished, her residuary legatee, I am convinced, is not the Nonconformist bodies, but the Papacy, the most cunningly contrived system of State polity the world has seen. Gladly and thankfully do I acknowledge the zeal, and piety, and services to Christian liberty of the Nonconformists ; but confessedly they have neither the antiquity, nor the prestige, nor the learning, nor the social position that would enable them to resist the swelling tide of Rome's advance. Sheltered under our lee, they have a freedom of worship and action to-day, which, were our position shattered, would be gone to-morrow. Many of them know it, and are honest enough to confess it. When the oak is felled, down comes the ivy.

Third. The Established Church secures the Protestant succession to the throne. What Englishmen have bought so dear, they will do well to keep.

Lastly, I would remind you that ours is a *Comprehensive Church ;* she admits within her pale High Churchmen and Broad Churchmen, as well as Low Churchmen. Nor would we have it otherwise; multitudes are thus brought in her services within the sound of the gospel who would turn their backs at once were she narrow and exclusive. But never forget that Truth exists independently of men's views of truth, and there are *limits* to her comprehensiveness. These limits are clearly defined in her Creeds, Articles, and Prayer-Book ; yet there is, beyond question, a strong party in our midst determined to widen those limits, if it possibly can, in the direction of Rome ; and if not, to overstep them. I hold it, therefore, the bounden duty of every Churchman to know why he is a Churchman, and what his Church holds and teaches ; and then with all loyal effort, and in the spirit of charity, to counteract the false doctrines so prevalent, and to preserve his Church. What that teaching is on certain vital matters, it will be my privilege to attempt to show you in these Lectures ; and may the Spirit of truth and love guide and bless the effort.

The Christian Ministry.

"When He ascended up on high, He led captivity captive, and gave gifts unto men. (Now that He ascended, what is it but that He also descended first into the lower parts of the earth? He that descended is the same also that ascended up far above all heavens, that He might fill all things.) And He gave some, apostles; and some, prophets; and some, evangelists; and some, pastors and teachers; for the perfecting of the saints, for the work of the ministry, for the edifying of the body of Christ."—EPH. iv. 9-12.

OUR subject last Sunday evening was the Church; I tried to show what it is and what it is not; I endeavoured to disengage the word "Church" from some of its present-day entanglements, and to show its true meaning. From this it was easy and delightful to point out how we as Churchmen are members of a visible community boasting the most venerable antiquity, a Church hard at work not only before the Reformation, but before Augustine landed on the shores of Kent, a Church that existed before king or Parliament, and that can trace back its lineage, if not to the apostles themselves, at least to the apostolic age; a sound branch of the Catholic Church, and its true historical representative in England to-day.

25

Now, such a Church must of necessity have an order of men set apart for the ministry of God's Word and Sacraments, and our text reminds us that this is a matter of nothing less than Divine provision. Translated literally, its terms are exceedingly suggestive. We are told on apostolic authority that Christ "ascended that He might give gifts unto men, . . . and He gave some *to be* apostles, and some prophets, and some evangelists, and some pastors who are teachers, with a view to the equipment of the saints for their work of service, for the upbuilding of the body of Christ." A duly ordained ministry is the gift of our ascended Lord to His Church. Some of these offices, as, for instance, those of the New Testament apostles and prophets, fell into abeyance as the need of them ceased to be felt. Others, again, not specified here, are familiar to us, and our Church in her Ordinal traces back her threefold order or bishop, priest, and deacon to apostolic times. Her assertion on this point is absolutely unquestioned as regards priests and deacons ; with regard to the Episcopate we are separated from the Presbyterian and certain other Churches. This question really lies within narrow limits. While in the New Testament the terms "bishop" and "presbyter" are often used interchangeably, being practically synonymous, and the Episcopal Order did not develope so long as the Apostolate remained ; yet it is an unquestioned historical fact that, within a hundred years of the apostles, we find Episcopacy universally recognised in every portion of the Church,[1] and even in the heretical sects seceding from it. Our Church, in maintaining the threefold order, is convinced of its Scriptural character ; but as the arguments for it are rather of the nature of intimations than of positive precept, she does not dare to un-church (to use Baxter's word) those who have all other marks of a true Church polity except Episcopacy. Hooker's great authority admits that, as in the case of Beza, there may be sometimes just and suffi- cient reason for allowing ordination made without bishops : " Men may be extraordi- narily but allowably admitted in two ways into spiritual functions in the Church. One is, when God Himself doth of Himself raise up any one; another is, when necessity doth constrain us to leave the usual ways of the Church, which otherwise we would willingly keep."

It is well known that that famous High Churchman, Bishop Cosin, of Durham, freely admitted this principle; and an Act passed in the 13th of Elizabeth (A.D. 1570) distinctly recog- nises the validity of Presbyterian and foreign orders ; requiring only that those non-episco- pally ordained should, in order to hold office in our Church, subscribe to the Articles before the bishop. Some of you know that the venerable Society for the Propagation of the

---

[1] As early probably as A.D. 110 we find Episcopacy mentioned in the Epistles of St. Ignatius as a well- ascertained fact of Church life in the many Churches to which he wrote. All early history seems to point to Asia, to Ephesus, to St. John, as its original source.

Gospel, with the bishops at its head, for many years employed German missionaries having Presbyterian and not Episcopal ordination, when it could obtain no others.

In view of matters which I shall immediately lay before you it is well to remember these facts. Let no man say, however, we think it matters not what order of ministry we have ; we cling to what we believe to have full Scriptural sanction ; and from the standpoint of history we vigorously maintain the threefold order to be essential, not to the being, but to the well-being of a Church ; but there is all the difference in the world between denying the *validity* and denying the *regularity* of orders. Our orders have both validity and regularity, others the former only. Since the year 1662 our Church has made Episcopal ordination obligatory on all her ministers ; in regard to other Churches differently constituted she is silent.

Now this brings us at once face to face with two matters that have assumed the highest importance, matters I am compelled to speak plainly about, although I do so with real reluctance. These are the questions of Apostolical Succession, and the nature of the Priesthood of the Church of England.

I. With regard to the first, while it is an undoubted fact that at no time since Christ has the Church been without a continuous ministry, linking (as do the Lord's Day and the Sacraments) the Church of to-day with that of Pentecost, the claim of Apostolical Succession goes considerably farther. It is the claim on behalf of our clergy of a lineal descent of power from the apostles, by virtue of a continued and unbroken succession of bishops in every effectual ordination. In so important a claim, involving so much, it is only right to let the High Churchmen speak for themselves.

Dr. Hook, the well-known Vicar of Leeds, writes thus in his Church Dictionary : " The Apostolic Succession is essential to the right administration of the holy sacraments. The clergy of the Church of England can trace their connexion with the apostles by links, not one of which is wanting, from the times of St. Paul and St. Peter to our own." The late Bishop of Winchester, Samuel Wilberforce, said, " The bishops of the Church of England are, by unbroken succession, the descendants of the original Twelve." Dean Goulburn declares : " There is, and there can be, no real and true church apart from the one society which the apostles founded, and which has been propagated only in the line of the Episcopal succession. There is no regular authority or right for the ministry whatsoever but only in this one line " (" Holy Catholic Church," p. 83).

These are tremendous claims. The validity of the Sacraments, as Mr. Gore terms it, nay, the very existence of the Church itself, is made to hang upon the Apostolical Succession. To a large number of our clergy those noble and inspiring words, "I believe one Catholic and Apostolic Church," mean *nothing* if they do not mean all this.

Now, assuming this doctrine to be true, we

may expect our Church to give forth no uncertain sound on the subject ; for, if true, it is
simply *vital* to her position.   The result,
then, of an examination of her Liturgy, her
Formularies, and her Articles, is somewhat
startling ; for, as Newman long ago was quick
to see, the Church of England is entirely
silent about any such Succession.   She
claims emphatically her historical position ;
she claims an apostolical ministry ; but she
bases her claim not upon any alleged Apostolical succession, but upon her faithfulness to
apostolic doctrine and practice.   Not even in
her Ordinal does she hint at such a Succession.   In her Twenty-fifth Article, indeed,
she declares that ordination is not a sacrament ; but if not, it must be a *tradition* or
a *ceremony*, and these the Thirty-fourth
Article pronounces " not necessary to be in
all places one and utterly alike."   In the
Twenty-third (part of which is word for word
the same as the Augsburg Confession) she
says positively : " We ought to judge those
lawfully sent, which be chosen to this work
by men who have public authority given
unto them in the congregation to call and
send ministers into the Lord's vineyard."   It
is useless to quibble over these words : the
Church of England, strong in her own un-
rivalled position, does *not* limit a lawful
ministry to those episcopally ordained.

    But the inherent weakness of the claim of
Apostolical Succession by the modern Anglo-
Catholic may easily be demonstrated in other
ways ; he has not his own Church behind

him ; has he anything else ? Let us see. I
want to make this matter perfectly plain, and
I would urge the following points :—

First, the man who makes this claim must
prove it. You of the laity should insist upon
this, for your eternal interests are declared to be
at stake. Do not think the usual answer
sufficient, that Christ ordained His apostles,
and promised to be with His Church to the
end of the age ; it is utterly insufficient.
Or that other answer, that He gave to His
apostles exclusively the authority to remit
sins ; it proves nothing if it were true ; but it
is not true, for, as Bishop Westcott points
out,[1] this authority was not given to the
Twelve only, but to the whole Society of the
Church, to the women as well as to the men.
Suppose that somebody were to claim succession to the Crown of England ; first and fore-
most he would have to prove his descent link
by link from our ancient sovereigns ; and I am
strongly of opinion that some other place
than Windsor would be his future abode if,
when challenged to produce his pedigree,
all he could urge was that constitutional
monarchy had always been the accepted
English form of government. Archbishop
Whately says distinctly : " There is not a
minister in all Christendom who is able with

[1] " There is nothing to show that the gift (of the Holy
Spirit) was confined to any particular group (as the
Apostles) among the whole company present. The com-
mission, therefore, must be regarded properly as the com-
mission of the Christian Society, and not that of the
Christian ministry."—*Speaker's Commentary*, John xx. 23.

any degree of certainty to prove his own
spiritual pedigree." Will you please remember what this claim actually comes to—
that all through the storm-tossed centuries of
the Church the *individual* clergyman is able
to trace, link by link, through a series of
properly ordained bishops, his own connexion,
by the laying on of hands, with the apostles
themselves! If one single link is missing, the
whole chain, yes, and all that hangs upon it,
falls to the ground ; and yet, as a matter of
fact, we do not know whether St. Peter, the
alleged first bishop of Rome, was ever in
Rome at all ; it is quite uncertain whether
Clement or Linus was the second ; and as to
the third, we are still more in the dark.

Again, let me remind you that since special
grace is said to be secured by this Succession
special results must follow—results perceptible
to men—or obviously the mere assertion of
them tends to bring the assertors into dis-
repute. Now, does Apostolic Succession make
its believers, or its supposed receivers, ex-
amples of peculiar grace ? Can we say that
the High Church party as a whole manifests, in
any special way, unworldliness either in church
or out of church ? Can we point to any particular zeal for the mission field ? Sad indeed it is to confess that hardly any hypothesis is so poorly supported by actual facts as
this. I would go further, and point out that
Apostolical Succession has never safeguarded
the Church from the greatest dangers that can
beset it. In the fourth century it did not
protect three-fourths of the Church from

adopting Arianism, the most deadly heresy that ever reared its head. The Roman Church insists, as you know, on exclusive Apostolic Succession ; and yet, in this nineteenth century of grace, it has not been kept from inventing the blasphemous dogmas of the Immaculate Conception of the Blessed Virgin, and the Papal Infallibility.

And yet again, speaking of the Roman Church reminds me of another inherent weakness of this vaunted theory. I mean its narrowness, its *uncatholicity*. The Churchman who bases his Churchmanship on it is obliged logically to regard the Roman Church as a co-ordinate and sister Church. But the Church of Rome contemptuously refuses his kiss of peace—she repudiates the Anglican Church as schismatic, its clergy she considers mere laymen, and its sacraments as null and void. She treats an English Churchman living in a Roman Catholic country as a heathen man ; he cannot communicate at her altars when living, and when he dies he must be buried with the burial of an ass. She ignores the whole Anglican communion ; its Primate is in her eyes simply a lay-evangelist and Privy Councillor ; she forbids her members to enter our churches. Well, what is the consequence to the Anglican ? Simply this. The Roman Church, which on the other side of the Channel he venerates as the Catholic Church, on this side he must treat as the Roman schism, or the "new Italian Mission," as Archbishop Benson called it the other day.

3

So that a Frenchman at Boulogne is held to be a good Catholic ; but when he crosses to Folkestone, without any change in his views, he is a schismatic! On the contrary, when an Anglican goes to reside in Paris he is logically bound to submit himself to the Archbishop of the diocese ; only, unfortunately, if he does so, he must renounce his Anglicanism, not merely during his sojourn abroad, but for good and all.[1] Nor need I pause to point out how entirely this Succession theory separates the Anglican at home from all those Nonconformist bodies in which undoubtedly the signs of a Church are wrought. He must treat them—and I am sorry to say he actually does — exactly as the Roman Church abroad treats him. His theory simply sacrifices him on his own altar—it leaves him *isolated in Christendom.*

But need I continue ? I have said enough to prove the doctrine of Apostolical Succession to be mechanical in operation, uncatholic in tendency ; it is not asserted in our Prayer-Book, it is certainly not found in the Bible, it is incapable of proof, it is the lowest Church view of the Ministry ever put forth—it is untrue.

[1] This point is excellently worked out by the Rev. R. E. Bartlett, in the *Contemporary Review* for March, 1893, from whom I borrow it. He amusingly illustrates thus : An Anglican and a Roman priest and a Nonconformist minister are shipwrecked together on a desert island. The Anglican congratulates his Roman brother that the Catholics are two to one. "Not at all," replies the Roman ; "you Protestants are two to one ; leave me alone, if you please ; I am the only Catholic."

II. I pass naturally, in the second place, to what springs out of this assumption, viz., the sacerdotal claims so strongly put forward on behalf of the second order of the ministry.

Let Mr. Bennett, Vicar of Frome, examined before the Ritual Commission, speak for his party. " Do you consider yourself a sacrificing priest ?—Yes. In fact, *sacerdos*, a sacrificing priest ?—Distinctly so. Then you think you offer a propitiatory sacrifice ?—Yes, I think I do offer a propitiatory sacrifice." It is needless to multiply evidence as to this claim. Only the other day the Bishop of Lincoln said (quite mistakenly, by the way) that the sacerdotal character of the priesthood was at stake in his trial. It is asserted by thousands of our clergy. " You should never speak of your priest as a minister or clergyman," is a rebuke not unfrequently heard.

Brethren, I call upon you as Christian men, if, indeed, you love Christ ; and as loyal sons of the Church of your baptism, to repudiate this assertion whenever made, and expose its hollowness ; it does infinite dishonour to Christ, it is likely to rend our Church in twain. Is it true, or is it false ? That is our business to discover to-day. We have three Courts of Appeal in this matter, and to each of them we will go.

The first is the Bible : and I challenge contradiction when I say that there is no single passage in the whole Scriptures in which the sacerdotal title is once given to the Christian minister, nor is the term "altar" once found as meaning the Lord's Table. I want you to search your Bibles on this matter. If English Churchmen knew the Scriptures better it would be better, depend upon it, for the English Church.

Our second court of appeal is to the Early Fathers. Dr. Pusey and his followers are fond of appealing to the Early Fathers. Let us appeal to the Fathers, too, but, mind you, it must be to the *early* Fathers : to Clement of Rome, to Ignatius, to Polycarp, to Justin Martyr, to Irenæus, to Clement of Alexandria ; and then what will you find ? Simply what Bishop Lightfoot has shown in his great " Dissertation on the Christian Ministry," examining these Fathers in detail, that each one and all of them is absolutely silent as to any sacerdotal claim pertaining to the Christian ministry. It is not till we come to the beginning of the third century that we find Tertullian putting forth these claims. He does so hesitatingly—in fact, he says in one passage, " Are not even we laics priests ? " evidently thinking of that word of St. Peter that, whether presbyter or layman, the Christian is a priest set apart "to offer up spiritual sacrifices unto God." It is not until we come to the time of Cyprian, in the middle of the same century, that for the first time we find these claims unhesitatingly put forward, claiming for the Christian ministry sacerdotal titles, functions, and powers, and from that day onwards there have always been those who have supported the claim. Well does our neighbour, the Rev. J. W. Marshall, say, that "to Cyprian belongs the responsibility of having introduced into God's vineyard this plant of human origin. That it found congenial soil was quickly proved by the amazing vigour with which it grew, corrupting the whole Church, shutting out poor sinners from the light of the gospel, substituting the priest for the Saviour, penance for repentance, and making merchandise of the souls of men, till God raised up Luther and Melancthon to lay the axe of God's truth to its root in Germany, and Cranmer, Ridley, and Latimer, and their followers to light such a fire in England as burned it to the ground."

But you will ask, reasonably enough, Whence did Cyprian get the seed of this noxious plant? The answer of the learned Bishop Lightfoot is instructive indeed. In the essay I have already quoted he says :— " The progress of the *sacerdotal* view of the ministry is one of the most striking and important phenomena in the history of the Church. . . . It is to Gentile feeling that this development must be ascribed. For the heathen, familiar with auguries, lustrations, and sacrifices, and depending upon the intervention of some priest for all the manifold religious rites of the State, the Club, and the Family, the sacerdotal functions must have occupied a far larger place in the affairs of every-day life than for the Jew of the Dispersion."

And again, "It is significant that the first instances of the term 'priest' applied to a Christian minister occurs in a heathen writer, Lucian." Thus this sacerdotal claim is

historically proved to be based not so much
on Judaism as on heathenism !

Our third court of appeal must, of course, be
to our own beloved Protestant and Reformed
Church, and she, thank God, in her Liturgy,
her Articles, her Canons, allows neither
priesthood nor sacrifice, if by priesthood be
meant ministers who can offer a propitiation
for sin, and by sacrifice be meant such an
offering. Is it really needful to repeat for the
hundredth time that our English word *priest*
comes immediately from the French word
prestre, or *prêtre,* itself a mere contraction of
presbyter, or elder ? Yes, I think it is, for
conversing the other day with an excellent
High Church clergyman, I found he was
entirely ignorant of this elementary fact.
Another clergyman was asked by a lady of
my acquaintance the meaning of the Greek
word "presbuteros," or presbyter, and he at
once replied, "A sacrificing priest"! Even
Mr. Sadler admits the actual name of priest
is never applied to a Christian minister.
Deeply do I lament, therefore, the ambiguity
of the word "priest" as we now have it in the
rubrics, for it suggests an idea of sacrifice it
was never intended to convey. When our
Prayer-Book was compiled we find the term
"minister" as its equivalent. Thus in the 32nd
Canon we read, "None is to be made a
deacon or minister in one day," and in the
76th Canon, "No man being admitted a
deacon or minister."

The fact is that sacerdotalism was deliberately set aside by our Church at the Refor-

mation, and nothing will convince you of this more readily than a comparison of our present Ordinal with the First and Second Prayer-Books of Edward VI. I want you to compare carefully the method of ordination before, during, and after the Reformation. Before the Reformation the bishop used these significant words, "Receive power to offer sacrifice to God, and to celebrate mass as well for the living as for the dead, in the name of the Lord." In 1550 (N.S.) these words were struck out, and the following were substituted: "Receive the Holy Ghost: whose soever sins ye remit, they are remitted; and whose soever sins ye retain, they are retained. Be thou a faithful dispenser of the Word of God and of His sacraments;" and a very suggestive rite was introduced, "the bishop shall deliver to every one of them the Bible in one hand, and the chalice, or cup, with the bread, in the other hand," for the first time drawing attention to the didactic or teaching character of the ministry. But in 1552 (N.S.) a further noteworthy change was introduced, the ordaining act and its accompanying words were allowed to stand, but the delivery of the chalice and paten were discontinued. The delivery of the Bible alone was preserved, our Church thus definitely *rejecting* the sacerdotal and exalting the didactic character of the presbyter.[1] He is declared to be a " pastor who is a teacher," in the terms of our text, and as such he is still the gift of Christ to His Church.

[1] See Dean Lefroy's " The Christian Ministry," p. 499.

With equal deliberation, and for the same purpose, the word "altar" which stained those two earlier Prayer-Books was removed, and "the Lord's Table," or "the Holy Table," substituted, in conformity with original and primitive use.

In short, to give you once more the un-answered learning of the late Bishop Light-foot, "The kingdom of Christ has *no sacer-dotal system*, and interposes no sacrificial tribe or class between God and man by whose intervention alone God is reconciled and man forgiven," and our Church solemnly and deliberately speaks accordingly.

I have kept you long. I am conscious I have shown you what the Christian ministry is not, rather than what it is, but the subject is of such absolute importance that I cannot feel I should have done otherwise. Enough at any rate has, I hope, been said to show that Apostolic Succession and a Sacerdotal Priest-hood form no part of a loyal Churchman's creed. At the Reformation, everything that expressed sacrifice or priestly function was swept away, and the primitive doctrine re-stored. All intelligent and loyal Churchmen were cheered the other day by words that fell from the lips of the Archbishop of Canterbury, as chairman of the annual meeting of the Society for the Propagation of the Gospel. Speaking of the Reformation, he said : "I seldom take up books or magazines but I see a silly carping at the Reformation. It has begun, and one sees it repeated. To my mind, the English Reformation—and I am as certain of the fact as I can be of anything—is the greatest event in Church history since the days of the apostles. It does bring back the Church of God to the primitive model." These are brave words nowadays, let them not be forgotten.

But to-night many of us are about to gather round the Table of our Lord, and I cannot let the sounds of controversy be the last before we draw near with faith. Here at least we are to remember that if we would receive this Holy Sacrament with benefit to our souls we are to be in perfect charity with all men. Do not forget, as I conclude this lecture, that false teaching such as we have dealt with is often based upon some essential longing of the human heart. We do need an altar ;—God has provided one ; we find it at " the place called Calvary." We do need a sacrifice ;—God has provided one—"the Lamb of God that taketh away the sin of the world." We do need something more than a presbyter, we need a priest : God has provided one, " a great High Priest, that is passed through the heavens ;" and unspeakably sad it would be for me, for you, if, while zealous to maintain apostolic doctrine within our beloved Church, we were ourselves found in that day to be unsprinkled by the blood of the one Sacrifice, not partakers of the one altar, not saved by the one Mediator between God and man ; while others, whose doctrine we rightly condemn, entered without us into the joy of our common Lord.

The Sacrament of Holy Baptism.

"Jesus answered, Verily, verily, I say unto thee, Except a man be born of water and of the Spirit, he cannot enter into the kingdom of God."—JOHN iii. 5.

THE Gospel Sacraments can hardly be rightly understood unless in connexion with the Sacramentalism of the older dispensation. They are parts of a Divine whole. From the earliest times, He, "whose delights are with the sons of men," has been pleased to enter into covenant with them, and in so doing He has usually vouchsafed some outward symbol or pledge of that blessed relationship. Perhaps the Tree of Life in Eden had such a significance to Adam ; beyond question the Bow in the cloud was of a sacramental nature to Noah ; so, too, the Sacrifices of the Law, and the rite of Circumcision given to Abraham before the Law. All these instances, with many others, illustrate the sacramental idea that a Divine Promise is in God's beneficent wisdom accompanied by a Divine Sign.[1] And when the Sun of Righteousness arose, and the shadows of the Old Covenant passed away, the Lord Jesus, again stooping to human need, gave His Church the two Sacraments,

[1] See Moule's "Outlines of Christian Doctrine."

the one of water Baptism, the other the bread and wine of the Eucharist.

As to the precise nature of these Sacraments our Church leaves us in no doubt, defining it with admirable clearness in her Article.

Here we learn that the Sacraments are *badges*, distinguishing Christian men from those who are not. In these days, when most are nominally Christian, this is lost sight of to a considerable extent; but in heathen or Mahomedan lands, or among Jews, perhaps the first thing evident in the Sacraments is that they are badges. How thrilling a sight to see a heathen, convicted of sin and led to Christ, publicly go down beneath those waters of death, the baptismal flood; and then coming forth, often with loss of parents, wife, children, and lands, declare himself to have been buried with Christ in baptism, and that henceforth he will fight manfully under His banner against sin, the world, and the devil, and continue Christ's faithful soldier and servant unto his life's end! And this may be seen daily in the mission field. But they are something more than badges—we are assured they are *witnesses*. And such they are, in an interesting way, to their own authenticity. Scattered in every part of the world, north and south, east and west, we find the Churches of Christ to-day. They differ from each other in constitution, pureness, and order; upon some matters they are even openly opposed; and yet all have this in common, that they possess these two Sacraments. How, and when, and where did they obtain them?

The question admits of but one answer. All these Churches are like so many radii of a wheel, each of which finds its proper starting-point in the Church at Jerusalem. In other words, they received them—the original institutions—from the hands of Him who ordained the Lord's Supper before He suffered, and Baptism before He ascended. No modern Church dare invent new sacraments; no ancient Church like Rome, that has actually done so, can hope to have them universally accepted. These two Sacraments thus testify to their own authenticity; they come directly from Christ Himself, and indirectly they witness to His death and resurrection as historical facts. But to most of you they are witnesses, I doubt not, in a far more personal and precious sense : they assure you, as you use them, of things unseen and eternal; they are visible pledges of the New Covenant, they are seals of your salvation, they attest to your inmost soul that its deepest needs are met. In this sense especially you acknowledge them as witnesses.

But they are more than witnesses; the Article says that they are *effectual signs.* In other words, God has been pleased to ordain and use the Sacraments as special channels of His grace. In His infinite love they are designed to be " a means whereby we receive the same," as well as "a pledge to assure us thereof." In the New Testament we find that the sign and the thing signified are constantly linked together. Thus, in Eph. v. 26, we are told, " Christ loved the

Church, and gave Himself for it, that He might sanctify and cleanse it with the washing of water by the word,"—that is, literally, "in an utterance," referring not to the Scriptures, but probably to the formula, "I baptize thee in the name of the Father, Son, and Holy Ghost ; " or, as some think, to the confession of faith by the candidate at the time of baptism. So, too, in Titus iii. 5 : " Not by works of righteousness that we have done, but according to His mercy He saved us, by the laver of regeneration, and renewing of the Holy Ghost." And yet again, in our text, the Lord beyond question refers to baptism when He says to startled Nicodemus, " Except a man be born of water and of the Spirit, he cannot enter into the kingdom of God."

But although the Scriptures thus link the sign and the thing signified together, are they always and inseparably connected ? Simon is a Scriptural proof and example that they are not. He who was baptized by the Evangelist as a believer is judicially declared by the Apostle to be still " in the bond of iniquity and in the gall of bitterness." And while our Prayer-Book, following the Scripture, links together the Sacraments and the grace they are designed to convey in general terms, it nevertheless dogmatically declares that the Sacraments are " generally " (that is, not universally) "necessary to salvation." Who, for instance, in the Western Church would say that the Eucharist was necessary for an infant ? And, as to Baptism, all that our own Church says in her comment on the gospel, in the Office of Baptism for such as are of Riper years, is "Whereby ye may perceive the great necessity of this sacrament, *where* it may be had."

This brings me at once, as you will see, into painful conflict with what I may without offence call the ordinary High Church view of baptism. That view is that the sign and the thing signified are always and invariably connected ; that the sign of water, and the germ or faculty of eternal life, are inseparable at the font. When some little time ago one had been truly converted, and came to tell his clergyman of his new-found peace and joy in the Holy Ghost, his response was, "It is the fruit of your baptism." "No, sir," was the reply, "that cannot be, for I have never been baptized, and I wanted to ask whether I ought not to be baptized now ; since, by God's grace, I have been born again." And I am sure that, as regards adult baptism, this story told by Mr. Moule just illustrates our own view. In our Confirmation classes I find now and again an unbaptized candidate : before Confirmation he must be baptized ; but of course I should never think of baptizing any one who did not give sufficient evidence of union with Christ by a living faith, and of forsaking sin in will and purpose. Adult baptism presents no difficulty, I suppose, to any of us.

The controversy really circles round the baptism of infants. It is not necessary for me to defend here the practice of infant baptism. I am not speaking to Baptists to-night, I am speaking to Churchmen. Yet it may be that deep down in the hearts of some there is a lingering doubt whether, after all, infant baptism is really according to the mind of Christ. " Give me a plain text," you would like to say, " that infants should be baptized." Willingly, my friends, if you will give me a plain text that the first day in the week should be observed as the Christian Sabbath. The fact is that the Scripture is silent about infant baptism, and its silence seems to me eloquent in its favour. I cannot bring myself to believe that He who promised to guide His Church into all truth should have permitted that Church for centuries to bring its little ones to baptism without a single injunction against it, or at least without bidding parents train and prepare their children for this sacrament. The repeated baptism of " households " by St. Paul is, to say the least, suggestive ; but to my own mind, if the initiatory rite of the New Covenant is *federal*, or covenanting, in its nature, the analogy of Circumcision, by which the Jewish parent sealed his child as a partaker of the Old Covenant, is simply irresistible. A converted Jew, remember, has never the slightest difficulty about infant baptism. He stumbles at the Incarnation, and the doctrine of the Tri-Unity ; but, these embraced, he brings his infant to the font without hesitation. Just as a Jewish proselyte was circumcised, and all his children with him, so in the Early Church it is almost certain that the baptism of a Jewish convert was accompanied by that of all his young children ; and you cannot doubt that

St. Paul had this in his mind when, in Col. ii. 11, 12, he distinctly calls baptism "the circumcision made without hands." Do not forget how, under the New Covenant, a child, even where one parent only is a believer, shares the privileges of that parent before God. " Else were your children unclean," says the Apostle, " but now are they holy " (1 Cor. vii. 14). "Ah, but," says one, " he that believeth and is baptized shall be saved ; a child cannot believe, and therefore cannot possibly receive the seal of faith." If you urge that, I will tell you that circumcision is expressly termed by St. Paul " a seal of faith," but I prefer simply to say that your text does not touch the question between us ; it obviously refers to adults. If there were a text that said no one was to be baptized unless he repented and believed, there would be an end of controversy ; but there is no such text.

  The question, then, before us is not whether infants may or may not be regenerated at baptism ; for God is a sovereign Lord, and He worketh as He wills ; but whether infants brought to the font do *invariably* and *always* receive, at least in germ, that grace of baptism defined as " a death unto sin and a new birth unto righteousness " ? The High Churchman answers, " Yes, they do ; " and quoting the words of our Office, " Seeing now that this child is regenerate, and grafted into the body of Christ's Church," he exclaims, "Here is what the Church says. This is enough for me. The Church declares this child to be regenerate ; further discussion is useless.'

This argument is chiefly remarkable for its simplicity. It is the Socinian's argument when he takes the words, " the man Christ Jesus," and says, " The Scripture plainly calls Him a man, I call Him a man too. The matter is settled." It is the Roman Catholic's argument when, urging the intercession of the Blessed Virgin, he has told me that our Lord did His first miracle at her request. It is the modern Anglican's argument about the words, " This is My Body," and He bows to a Presence in the elements and worships. This argument applied to baptism, however, will not do for intelligent Christians or well-taught Churchmen. Unfair in itself, it entirely ignores two things. One, the fundamental principle on which the whole Prayer-Book is constructed ; the other, the essential conditions on which alone infants are baptized. To both these I invite your particular attention.

I. In the first place, then, I hold that *the High Church view wholly overlooks the fundamental principle of the Prayer-Book.* That principle is simply this, that our Church in her Liturgy takes men on their own showing and profession. Those who " profess and call themselves Christians " she treats in her public services as such. Hence, from the moment she welcomes them into the House of God as, " Dearly beloved brethren," to the day when she lays them in the dust, " in sure and certain hope of eternal life," she does so on their own responsibility, and uses language suitable to the calling they profess.

But our compilers never for one moment

4

thought that all who joined in her services
would be really and truly Christians. Their
object was to construct a Liturgy for believers, and for believers only ; and they
used the highest language suitable to such.
It must be plain to you that they could not
compile two Service-books, one for believers,
and the other for unbelievers ; for the latter
would never be used by those for whom it
was intended, and *could* never be used by any
one else. Some Nonconformists (not all)
object altogether to a Liturgy. It is wrong,
they say, to put a Book of Common Prayer
into the hands of a mixed congregation,
partly Christian, partly non-Christian. Well,
will they who say so defend their own universal practice of putting into the hands of
mixed congregations Books of Common
Praise ? In thousands of chapels, as well
as of churches, there are saved and unsaved
together to-night, and they are singing together words like these—

> " Sun of my soul, Thou Saviour dear,
>   It is not night if Thou art near ;
>   O may no earth-born cloud arise,
>   To hide Thee from Thy servant's eyes."

Those who object, I say, to a Book of Common Prayer, must explain how it is they
adopt a Book of Common Praise. The
rhyme can hardly account for it !

Our Baptismal Service is therefore designed
for the use of *Christian* parents and *Christian*
sponsors. Our Church reminds us that our
Lord took little unbaptized children into His

arms, laid His hands upon them, and blessed them ; she bids us "earnestly believe that He will likewise favourably receive this present infant," brought in the arms of faith to Him. She leads us to pray definitely that He would "sanctify this water to the mystical (*i.e.*, the symbolical) washing away of sin ;" in other words, that He would be pleased to join the inward baptism of His Spirit with the outward baptism of water. The child is then named, as was the Jewish child at circumcision. And now, the act of immersion, or of affusion, being completed, our Church proceeds charitably to use the language of faith, " Seeing now that this child is regenerate." She takes it for granted that minister, parents, and sponsors have offered that prayer which Christ says entitles us to " believe that we have received it," [1] and, I put it to you who know the power of prayer, would you have it otherwise ? The misuse of this Sacrament surely does not invalidate its use ; but remember the important words of Archbishop Ussher, "Though we, *in the judgment of charity*, do judge this of every particular

---

[1] " I say unto you, All things whatsoever ye pray and ask for, believe that ye have received them, and ye shall have them " (Mark xi. 24, R.V.). " This is the boldness which we have toward Him, that, if we ask anything according to His will, He heareth us ; and if we know that He heareth us whatsoever we ask, we know that we have the petitions which we have asked of Him " (1 John v. 14, 15, R.V.). On this Bishop Westcott well says, He who takes God's will as his own, has all he seeks truly in present possession, though visible fulfilment be delayed.

infant, yet we have no ground to judge so of all in general ; or, if we judge so, it is *not any judgment of certainty—we may be mistaken.*" Was it not in this very spirit of charitable presumption that our Lord bade His disciples, " Into *whatsoever* house ye enter, first say, Peace be to this house ; and if the son of peace be there, your peace shall rest upon it ; if not, it shall turn to you again " ?   Was it not in this very spirit of our Liturgy that St. Paul wrote of all the Galatian Church what we know was only true of some, " As many of you have been baptized into Christ, have put on Christ " ? Do not his Epistles throughout breathe the same spirit ?

But, as for maintaining that the compilers of our Liturgy held that the mere act of baptism itself regenerated invariably and in every case, this is simply to maintain that they were fools.   I can use no weaker word.   It throws everything into confusion.   It makes them contradict altogether that Bible of which they had such a magnificent knowledge.   It makes them contradict their own Articles, every word of which they so carefully weighed and balanced ; for instance, the Twenty-fifth Article which says of the Sacraments, " In such only as *worthily* receive the same, they have a wholesome effect or operation ; " and the Twenty-sixth, which, speaking of the unworthiness of ministers, declares that " The grace of God's gifts is not diminished from such as *by faith and rightly* do receive the Sacraments ministered unto them ; " and the

Twenty-seventh, which says, " They that receive Baptism *rightly* are grafted into the Church," while " the promises of forgiveness of sins," and the like, " are visibly signed and sealed."

It makes them contradict their own published writings. Hear, for instance, the words of Cranmer, the Archbishop : " In baptism, those that come feignedly, and those that come unfeignedly, both be washed with sacramental water ; but both be not washed with the Holy Ghost, and clothed with Christ." And again, " All that wash with water be not washed with the Holy Ghost." But I need not trouble you with more quotations ; the words of the great Hooker, the recognised interpreter of the Prayer-Book, sum up the views of its authors, when he says, " All receive not the grace of God who receive the sacraments of His grace."

I claim, then, to have sufficiently shown that our grand old Liturgy is formed on a well-known hypothetical principle, and that this explains its language here, and is due to the very necessities of our public services. If anything were needed to confirm this, it is sufficient to remind you that our Reformers, almost without exception, held strongly the views of Calvin as to Election, Predestination, and Final Perseverance—a fact which makes it *utterly impossible* for them to have held the High Church view that all the baptized were *ex opere operato* regenerated. Dr. Mozley, the late Regius Professor of Divinity in the University of Oxford, is an unquestioned authority ; he strongly disliked the famous Gorham Judgment,[1] and determined to prove the view I am upholding untenable ; but as he studied the history of the Prayer-Book, he became convinced it was the view of its compilers ; and in his great work on the Primitive Doctrine of Baptismal Regeneration, he writes (page 102) : " Every child is, upon his baptism, asserted to be regenerate. The present chapter has decided the sense in which these statements are to be understood, viz., that they are *hypothetical.* It has also met the objections made to this mode of interpretation, as not being literal. I will only repeat here that the real question is, not what is the literal interpretation of these statements, but what is the *true* one. These statements in our formularies come before us with a certain history appended to them : these are *old* statements which have descended from prophets to apostles, from apostles to fathers, and from fathers age after age downwards, till at last we find them in our Prayer-Book and ritual. These state-

[1] The Bishop of Exeter, Dr. Philpotts, had refused to institute Mr. Gorham to the living of Brampford-Speke, on the ground that he denied spiritual regeneration to be the invariable accompaniment of infant baptism, holding that baptism is an effectual sign of grace, by which God works invisibly in us, but only in such as worthily receive it ; and, in fact, that regeneration may be given before, in, or after, baptism. The only question for the highest court was whether this doctrine was contrary or repugnant to the teaching of the Church of England. It was held to be not so contrary or repugnant.

ments must not, therefore, be isolated, separated from all interpretative data, and judged
of by themselves. They must be interpreted
in connection with their history, and in connection with previous language. The asserted
regeneration of the whole body of the baptized is but the continuation of the asserted
righteousness of the holy nation in the Old
Testament, and the asserted glory of the
Christian Church in the New. Is that assertion of Scripture, then, a literal or hypothetical
one? If the latter, then is the one in our
formularies hypothetical too.

The term ' regenerate' comes down to us
with a particular meaning stamped upon it,
which we cannot remove, according to which
it cannot possibly be asserted literally of all
baptized persons. *This is therefore an hypothetical assertion.*"

II. I hold, in the second place, that the High
Church view of infant baptism *altogether
overlooks the definite conditions* on which
alone such baptism is administered. It is
said by some High Churchmen that the grace
of God is certain in the case of the baptism
of infants, because, being unconscious, they
cannot put any obstacle or bar in the way or
His grace. But a mere negative condition
like this can never take the place of the condition of a living faith ; and, as I will show,
a living faith is the essential condition on
which the sacrament becomes efficacious.
The hypothesis of the Catechism and Confirmation Service alike is that the baptized
child is now actually and truly a believer.

"What is required by persons to be baptized?" asks our catechism (required, that is, by God, for our Church will of course take in such a matter no guidance but that of God Himself); and the answer is: "Repentance, whereby they forsake sin, and faith, whereby they steadfastly believe the promises of God made to them in that Sacrament." "Why, then, are infants baptized when, by reason of their tender age, they cannot perform them?" —and I would have you here to notice the difference between the catechism of 1604 and that of 1662, our present version. In 1604 the answer to this question was this: "Yes, they do perform them by their sureties, who promise and vow them both in their names, which, when they come of age, themselves are bound to perform." Here, you see, there was a substitution of the faith of the sponsors for the personal faith of the infant. That misleading answer was removed in 1662, and we find it as we have it now—" Because they promise them both by their sureties, which promise, when they come of age, themselves are bound to perform." The change is in itself exceedingly significant.[1] The words of Dr. Wall, who was thanked by Convocation in 1705 for his "History of Infant Baptism,"

[1] From the end of the second century, a time of martyrdom, the Church of God has provided sponsors as safeguards that the child given to Him may be brought up as God would have it brought up. But sponsors are not of Divine institution, nor does our Church hold them to be necessary; in the Private Baptism of Infants no sponsors are required, and yet similar words of faith and charity are used as in their public baptism.

are altogether relevant. He says this : " I say it appears to have been the meaning of the Church in that question and answer, not to determine whether infants are to be baptized, but to determine whether infants that are baptized are baptized upon any other covenant than that upon which grown persons are baptized—namely, of repentance and faith. And it determines that they are not baptized on any other but the very same, only with this difference, that the adult person is baptized into the hope of the kingdom of heaven, in which he does believe, and an infant is baptized on condition that he do, when he comes to age, believe."

"We baptize infants," says Mr. Moule, "because of the Covenant ; we study the Covenant and its terms and seals in the adult." It is into the lips of one thus "come to age " that our Catechism puts that much misunderstood answer to " Who gave you this name ? " viz., " My godfathers and my godmothers in my baptism, wherein I was made a member of Christ, a child of God, and an inheritor of the kingdom of heaven." This answer, I beg you remember, is not given by any ordinary child picked up at random. This answer is given by a "person," [1] before Confirmation, carefully instructed, and having an intelligent faith, one who can say, " I believe in God the Father, who hath made me and all the world ; in God the Son, who hath redeemed me and all man-

---

[1] See Title of Catechism.

kind ; and in God the Holy Ghost, who
sanctifieth me and all the elect people of
God." This is one of whom it is distinctly
affirmed in the Confirmation Service, which
usually precedes the first communion, that
he has been "regenerated by water and the
Holy Ghost, and has received forgiveness of
all his sins." The person, then, who gives
this answer is one who, well knowing what
grace is, and the Saviour's love, traces back
the Spirit's work to his baptismal dedication
—to that memorable hour when these bless-
ings, claimed for him in humble boldness
of faith, were assured to him by the seal of
the baptismal covenant ; and who now declares publicly that he *has fulfilled* the two-
fold condition on which he was then admitted
to its privileges.

A document familiar to lawyers, called an
Escrow, well illustrates this.[1] An escrow is
an instrument of gift, duly signed and sealed,
and in it is an agreement that the gift shall
not pass to the grantee unless some certain
condition is fulfilled ; and until that condition
is fulfilled, although the gift be in words
immediate, it cannot pass to the person for
whom it is designed. So soon as the condition
is fulfilled, then, without any further signing
or sealing, the instrument takes effect, and the
gift passes to the grantee. Just so in infant
baptism : the pledge of the covenant is "a
death unto sin, and a new birth unto righteousness ; " but equally clearly and distinctly are

---

[1] See Chancellor Warren's " Ex opere operato."

the conditions laid down of faith and repentance ; nor, until that faith and repentance
are given, is the Sacrament complete—till
then there is no true baptism ; and surely
that is what St. Peter meant when he said :
"Baptism doth also now save us (not the
putting away of the filth of the flesh, but the
answer of a good conscience towards God)."

Mr. Moule, whom all recognise as a
teacher, calls attention, as deeply significant,
to these words of Archbishop Ussher in the
beginning of the seventeenth century : "We
may judge that baptism is not actually
effectual to justify and sanctify until the
party do believe and embrace the promises.
Baptism is a seal of the righteousness of
Christ to be extraordinarily applied by the
Holy Ghost if an infant die in his infancy ;
to be apprehended by faith if he live to the
years of discretion. So that baptism administered to those of years is not effectual unless
they believe. We can make no comfortable
use of our baptism in infancy *until we believe.*"

I say, then, that the ordinary High Church
view entirely overlooks the conditions on
which infant baptism is vouchsafed in our
Church. Unintentionally, no doubt, but
really, this doctrine ties down a supreme act
of omnipotence to the will of man. The
minister, parents, and sponsors, may all be
infidel at heart ; no single prayer may have
ascended to the One Giver of grace ; the
child may grow up in utter ungodliness, as,
alas ! thousands of baptized children actually
do ; he may never exhibit a spark of spiritual

life—and as he has lived so he may die—yet, simply because, owing to the circumstances of his birth, he was brought in infancy to the font, this man is declared to have been once regenerate, a child of God, and an heir of the kingdom!   Not thus does the Holy One make demands upon our faith.   If so preposterous a theory were not upheld and vigorously insisted on by men of undoubted piety and learning, it would long ago have tumbled to pieces by the very absurdity of its own · pretensions.   Unfortunately it is so held and taught, and from my inmost soul I believe it to be simply deadly in its effects.   It has, in my opinion, distinctly lowered the standard of Christian life among a large section of Churchmen.   The six marks of the new birth given by the Holy Spirit in St. John's Epistles, " without which whosoever liveth is counted dead before God," are largely forgotten ; and, in many churches, one would judge the only essentials to be the two sacraments.   If baptized, men and women are invited without discrimination to the Eucharist, and the sacred bread and cup of the covenant are put, without warning,[1] into the hands of those who still are unquickened.

But I must not leave my subject—a controversial and therefore painful one—without a word of practical inquiry.   Some men speak as if there was really no alternative between

[1] " It is requisite that no man should come to the Holy Communion but with a full trust in God's mercy, and with a quiet conscience."—*Exhortation in Communion Service.*

the High Church theory of Regeneration and mere Registration! I would have you remember that in your Baptism in infancy you entered upon a position of great Privilege, of gracious Opportunity, of growing Responsibility. And just because it was so, I would ask in all solemn earnestness whether you, individually, have entered into that grace which, with humble boldness of faith, was claimed for you and assured to you in your baptism? Have you experienced a death unto sin, and a new birth unto righteousness? Symbolically, at any rate, you have been " buried by baptism into death, that, like as Christ was raised up from the dead by the glory of the Father, even so you also should walk in newness of life." Is this your actual experience? Have you by faith identified yourselves with Him who on Calvary identified Himself with you? If you have thus truly ratified your covenant connexion with Christ in His death, sure I am that, more or less fully, you are rejoicing in the power of His resurrection-life. Of such does Hooker finely say, " Blessed for ever and ever be that mother's child whose faith has made him the child of God. The earth may shake,—the pillars of the world may tremble under us,—the countenance of the heavens may be appalled,—the sun may lose his light, the moon her beauty, the stars their glory ; but, concerning the man that has trusted in God, what is there in the world that shall change his heart, overthrow his faith, alter his affection toward God, or the affection of God to him ? "

The Sacrament of the Lord's Supper.

" And He took bread, and gave thanks, and brake, and gave unto them, saying, This is My Body which is given for you : this do in remembrance of Me. Likewise also the cup after supper, saying, This cup is the New Covenant in My Blood, which is shed for you."—LUKE xxii. 19, 20.

OUR subject is confessedly a difficult one. Its difficulty is exceeded only by its importance. Right views of the Lord's Supper lie at the bottom of a great deal of our spiritual life, and you will expect me, as your clergyman, to show clearly what I think these views ought to be. We are separated from the Church of Rome upon this question more than upon any other. Our Reformers died to uphold the doctrine of the Church ot England, and yet to-day—I say it with unspeakable sadness—it is evident that Churchmen are almost hopelessly divided upon it. I cannot attempt to say anything new on a subject which has been debated for centuries. I shall be thankful if I can say a little of what is old ; for, in this case, as in so many others, the old is better.

One enormous advantage we have in this matter is that we can all easily refer to the inspired documents which contain the historical facts. This is no question that turns upon some ancient manuscript locked up in the libraries of Constantinople or Alexandria. The sources of information are equally accessible to us all. The nature and design of the Lord's Supper are stated with seemingly absolute clearness in the four accounts of its institution as we find them in the Gospels of St. Matthew, St. Mark, St. Luke ; and in St. Paul's First Epistle to the Corinthians.

Putting these together, they read thus : " The Lord Jesus, the same night that He was betrayed, as they were eating, took bread, and gave thanks, and blessed it, and brake it, and gave it to His disciples, and said, Take, eat ; this is My Body which is given and broken for you : this do in remembrance of Me. After the same manner, also, He took the cup when He had supped, and gave thanks, and gave it to them, saying, Drink ye all of it, for this is My Blood of the New Covenant which is shed for many for the remission of sins. This do, as oft as ye drink it, in remembrance of Me, for as oft as ye eat this bread and drink this cup, ye do show ('ye proclaim,' R.V.) the Lord's death till He come."

The meaning of these words, however, is disputed, or at least of some of them ; and the question among Churchmen and others is simply this—What is the meaning of Christ's words, "This is My Body," "This is My Blood," and how are we to feed upon them ?

I. I shall venture to lay down three propositions for our guidance :—

The first is this, We must take our Lord's words, " This is My Body," in the most literal and obvious sense they will bear. We may be thankful that on this point Roman and Anglican, High Church and Low Church, are perfectly agreed. Dr. Pusey says, " All things combine to make us take our Lord's words solemnly and literally." Archdeacon Wilberforce says, " That our Lord's words of institution were to be taken in their simple and natural sense, was the belief of all ancient writers." Prebendary Sadler, in the middle of a long argument against both the Roman and Protestant view, says, curiously, " Our only safe way is to adhere implicitly to the terms used in Scripture, without attempting to explain these hard sayings, and to leave them where Christ left them—in impenetrable obscurity." Is Ignorance, then, really the mother of Devotion ? Did I share his view as to their impenetrable obscurity, I should hardly follow his practice in attempting to explain them. But I do not ; I believe that those words, like all our Master uttered, are for the reverent and intelligent use of His Church. Let us see how they are interpreted :

Two quotations from the decrees of the Council of Trent will suffice to set forth the Roman view :—

" If any one denieth that in the Sacrament of the most Holy Eucharist are contained truly, really, and substantially, the Body and Blood, together with the soul and divinity of our Lord Jesus Christ, and consequently the whole Christ, but saith He is only therein symbolically, figuratively, or virtually, let him be anathema."

And again, " Christ, whole and perfect, is under the species of bread, and under every particle of it ; and whole under the species of wine, and every particle of it." In other words, " This *has under its species* My Body," is the Roman explanation of "This is My Body."

Two quotations will similarly show what is the Ritualistic view. In the "Little Prayer-Book" is this direction : " At the words, 'This is My Body,' 'This is My Blood,' you must believe that the bread and wine become the real Body and Blood, with the soul and Godhead of Jesus Christ ; bow down your head and body in deepest adoration when the priest says these awful words, and worship your Saviour then verily and indeed present on His altar " (p. 18).

Hear next what Dr. Pusey and the leading English Ritualists say in a solemn memorial to the Archbishop of Canterbury, to which their signatures are attached : " We believe that in the Holy Eucharist, by virtue of con-secration, through the power of the Holy Ghost, the body and blood of our Saviour Christ—'the inward part or thing signified' —are present really and truly, but spiritually and ineffably, under ' the outward visible part or sign,' or *form* of bread and wine."

So, to put the Ritualistic view in a sen-tence, " This is My Body " means "This *has under its form the presence of* My Body."

Placing our Lord's words and those of

these interpreters one below the other, we find they read thus :—

Bible	This	is...............	My Body.
R.C.	This	*has under its species ...*	My Body.
Ritualist ...	This	*has under its form the presence of*	My Body.

I appeal to you whether either of these sentences is at all a literal and obvious equivalent of the word "is." We shall presently find that the most literal meaning the Divine words will bear condemns at once both the Roman and the modern Anglican interpretation.

We can now advance a step further. My second proposition is this : We must take *all* the words Christ used if we would understand them. The full words are, " This is My Body which is given for you," " This is My Blood which is shed for you." Mark those words, " Which is given for you," " Which is shed for you," for much depends upon them.

Now the Roman Catholic, in consecrating the bread, says these words only : " Hoc est corpus meum " (" This is My Body "); and Bellarmine, in his treatise on the Eucharist, has a chapter on these words, in which he takes no notice of the rest of the sentence. Luther, in like manner, built his argument at Marburg on these words only, writing them, as we recollect, on the table before him. The same thing may be said of the High Churchmen now :—

Wilberforce's "On the Doctrine of the Eucharist" is a well-known book; but, as the learned Dr. Vogan points out, he practically omits just what the Roman Church and the Lutheran Church omit; "let any one," he says, "who is in possession of the book, take and blot out every place in which the words, 'Which is given for you,' 'Which is shed for you,' are recited, and he will find that they have not the least influence upon the argument and the doctrine which it is used to enforce." Now what is the result of this omission? Simply this: that the Roman Church, the Lutherans, and the Ritualists all take "This is My Body" to mean "This is My *glorified* Body." The Romanist defines the body in the Sacrament as "His true Body which was broken for us, and sitteth at the right hand of the Father in heaven, and is to die no more"—in other words, Christ's glorified Body. Dr. Pusey says, "Why should we think it too strange a thing for His marvellous condescension that He should now give us His blessed Body and Blood under the form of bread and wine, or how should His Body which He gives us not be His living, life-giving Body?" So, again, Archdeacon Wilberforce thus argues the presence of our Lord's Body to be possible: "Our Lord's human Body," he says, "is not subject to the laws of material existence, because His Body is a glorified Body, which has new qualities gained by oneness with Deity." In other words, it is Christ's glorified Body.

Again, let us put under each other the

Bible sentences and these interpretations of them :—

Bible......This	is	MyBodywhich *is given* for you.
R. C.......This	has under its species ...	My *glorified* Body.
Lutheran This	has with it	My *glorified* Body.
Ritualist This	has under its form the presence of	My *glorified* Body.

Plainly, therefore, whereas Christ referred to His Body as about to be crucified, the views before us refer to it as glorified, and do it by omitting to assign any meaning to the words, " Which is given for you," " Which is shed for you." On this ground, therefore, we are compelled to say that, taking *all* the words of the institution, the Bible gives no support to the Roman doctrine of Transubstantiation on the one hand, or to the High Church theory of Consubstantiation on the other.[1]

Our third proposition is as follows :—That the bread and wine are the Body and Blood

[1] Hence the growing practice among the Ritualistic clergy of omitting the words, " which was given for thee," " which was shed for thee ; " as they administer the bread and wine respectively. Notice that in these words our Church uses the past tense.

of our Lord now *in the same sense* in which they were His Body and Blood on the night of institution. This is absolutely important, and I will give you a few quotations in support of it.

St. Augustine says : " He gave to the disciples the Supper consecrated with His own hands, but we have not sat down to that banquet, and yet we daily eat the Supper itself by faith. Paul was not there who believed, Judas was there who betrayed. How many now, too, in this same Supper, though they saw not then that table, nor beheld with their eyes, nor tasted with their mouths, the bread which the Lord carried in His hands, yet, because *it is the same which is now prepared*, how many also in this Supper eat and drink judgment to themselves ! "

St. Chrysostom says : " This table is the same as that and nothing else." And again, " The first table hath no advantage above that which cometh after."

This, indeed, is one of our most cherished and fundamental privileges in that sacred feast, that "it is the same as that and nothing else," nothing less and nothing more. Handed down to us all through the long-drawn ages of the Church's life, it is still substantially the same as that instituted by our great Head Himself. Destroy this assurance, and what have we left ? But I say confidently that if the Roman and so-called Anglican doctrines of a Real Objective Presence be true, then the Lord's Supper now is *not* the same as that, it is something essentially different. Both these doctrines, I repeat, assert the Presence in the elements to be that of Christ's *glorified* Body. If so, then assuredly it is not the same Supper, for Christ's Body was *not* yet *glorified* on the night of institution. Is it, then, His crucified Body? But neither was Christ's Body yet broken for our sakes. Do you not see? Christ's Body as glorified and Christ's Body as crucified *were not* at the time of institution, and there can be no substantial presence of that which *is not.* I go further, and say that these doctrines not merely destroy the identity of our Eucharist with that, but they violate the very laws of thought. I put it to you, as intelligent Christian people, whether it is not an outrage upon faith and understanding alike, to say that while Christ was, beyond all possibility of doubt, sitting personally and bodily at that Holy Table, He was Himself, body, soul, and divinity; really, truly, and substantially; in the bread and wine? Yet this, and nothing but this, is what both the Roman and Ritualistic doctrines of the Real Objective Presence necessarily involve.

So far, then, for my task—a distasteful one at the best. These three propositions are so simple and obvious that they merely require stating, to commend themselves, I believe, to every candid mind; but use them carefully, and above all things in the spirit of Christian love, and you will save some perplexed and devout souls from fundamental error upon a matter of the most grave and sacred importance.

II. I should like to pass on at once to the

positive teaching of our Church upon what the disputed sentences do mean, but I must touch upon two or three points on the way.

Frequently, until it is a commonplace of many—I was almost going to say of most—pulpits, you will hear the Lord's Supper spoken of as a sacrifice. I have already shown, conclusively, I hope, in my lecture on the Christian ministry, that there is no or-dained sacerdotal priesthood mentioned in either the New Testament, the Prayer-Book, or the earliest Fathers ; and if there is no priest there can be no sacrifice, and if there is no sacri-fice there can be no altar. I will now merely add this, that in the New Testament the word " altar " occurs sixteen times, and not once is it used of the Lord's Table. In every case, with-out exception, it refers to the then existing Jewish altars."[1] The only earthly altar, says

[1] Heb. xiii. 10, " We have an altar whereof they have no right to eat who serve the tabernacle," is disputed. " By these words St. Paul (?) meant the Communion Table. By these words I mean the Communion Table." Thus, to my astonishment, I heard a well-known Presbyterian minister commence his sermon in St. Giles's Cathedral, Edinburgh. Many High Churchmen, unfortunately, agree with him, reminding us that texts apart from con-text are sometimes dangerous things. What do these words mean? The context explains. The Hebrew Christians, who still clung to the Temple and its services, felt that in their separation from its majestic and venerable ritual their very souls were bereaved. The writer, whose keynote throughout is "better," reminds them, therefore, in ver. 9 of the fundamental truth that "the heart is established by grace, not by meats," and he proceeds to prove this from the Law itself. Himself a Hebrew, he links himself with them ; " We (Hebrews) have an altar (viz. that of the yearly Sin-Offering), whereof they have

Bishop Westcott, " is the Cross upon which Christ offered Himself." The same great scholar writes : " In the first stage of Christian literature there is not only no example of the application of the word ' altar ' to any concrete material object as the Holy Table, but there is no room for such an application." It is noteworthy that even Mr. Sadler has to confess that " the Eucharist has *scarcely one thing in common* with what the Scriptures and English Churchmen commonly call sacrifice," although he adds immediately that it does possess " the most intense sacrificial reality," which looks very much as if he did not intend to be guided by one or the other.

Is it not, then, simply heart-breaking to those who, like ourselves, love their Church and

no right to eat who serve the tabernacle." This was a fact, and on it hinges his argument. Of that great Offering, so pregnant with meaning, and rich with blessing for a whole year, the priests could not partake as they did of other "altars," "*for*"—the reason was familiar to them all—"the bodies of those beasts are burned without the camp." Whatever blessing, then, there was in that great sacrifice must have been by "grace" alone, for "meats" there were none. But Jesus Christ being unchangeably the same (ver. 8), let them hold to the old doctrine (ver. 9). The writer's brethren were not deprived of grace, because they were deprived of ritual and sacrifice ; nay, it was outside the whole camp of Jewish ceremonial that the One great Sin-Offering, the Crucified, would be found, and if they wanted grace now they would only find it by going outside to Him. The reader has but to substitute the words "Communion Table" with the High Churchman, or " Cross of Christ " with many Low Churchmen, for the word "altar" in the text, to find that either brings the passage as a whole into confusion.

love their Bibles to know that literally thousands of devoted clergymen like Mr. Sadler are strenuously teaching, by sermon and lecture, by ritual and symbol, that the priesthood of the English Church is not merely ministerial but sacerdotal, that the Lord's Table is really an altar, and that they offer on it a real sacrifice ?

Dr. Pusey, like many of his followers, argued that the words, " Do this in remembrance of Me," really mean, "Sacrifice this in remembrance of Me." Such a use of the Greek verb would be absolutely unique in the New Testament. Bishop Thirlwall was the greatest Greek scholar of his time, and his comment was alike caustic and suggestive : " Dr. Pusey may say so, but I do not think he will find any Greek scholar or any sound theologian to agree with him."

Yet again, you may constantly hear our Lord's solemn words in John vi. 53–57 quoted as if He then referred to the Eucharist, and to nothing else. I read a recent sermon by the Dean of St. Paul's, in which he said to the congregation indiscriminately, " Turn not your backs upon that heavenly feast, concerning which Christ said, ' Whoso eateth My flesh and drinketh My blood hath eternal life, and I will raise him up at the last day.' " Now, at the risk of seeming presumption, I must honestly confess that I am unable to see even an allusion to the Lord's Supper in Christ's words, much less a direct reference such as the Dean asserts, and for the following good and sufficient reasons. First, taken thus they would prove too much. They would prove that even Judas, and every bad man who has come to that Holy Table ever since, had eternal life—an awkward conclusion, surely. In the second place, I find that our Lord was addressing unconverted Jews, but His Supper is meant, as you will freely admit, only for baptized Christians. Thirdly, the Sacrament was not even in existence, nor was it so for some twelve months later. Such a threefold cord is not easily broken. No, never does our Lord make salvation dependent upon any Sacrament. The Sacraments were not meant to impart life, but to maintain life. The real connexion between that profound discourse and the Lord's Supper is this, that both set forth—the one in words, the other in a Divine object-lesson—the same essential truth, that the soul that desires salvation must feed upon Christ. *Crede et manducasti* (" Believe, and thou hast eaten ") is Augustine's summing up of this view in one luminous sentence. Our Church enforces the same principle when, in the Communion for the Sick, she bids the curate instruct the patient in the extremity of his sickness that, if he do truly repent, and believe that Christ his Saviour died upon the Cross for his redemption, " he doth eat and drink the Body and Blood of our Saviour Christ profitably to his soul's health, although he do not receive the sacrament with his mouth."

I cannot now pause upon the doctrine of the Extension of the Incarnation. Many of you have never heard of it. It rests upon a half truth, but is untrue as a whole. I must pass on to St. Paul's words in the eleventh chapter of the First Epistle to the Corinthians : " He that eateth and drinketh unworthily eateth and drinketh damnation to himself, not discerning the Lord's Body." These words perplex many, but look at them in the Revised Version, and especially in connexion with the context, and you will see at once that they have nothing whatever to do with any supposed Presence in the elements. The " body " here is simply the Church, and the teaching, too often forgotten still, is that he who comes to the Lord's Table selfish, and forgetful of his oneness in Christ with all Christ's people, partakes to his own condemnation. This explains the remedy proposed in the last two verses of the chapter.

III. What, then, is the meaning of "This is My Body " ? To myself it is perfectly certain, from the context in the three Gospels, that the word " is " can only be used in a particular sense. For observe, the words are not merely " This is My Body," but " This cup is the New Covenant in My Blood." Why insist on a literal meaning in the former sentence when a literal meaning is impossible in the latter ? " Is " can only mean *represents* in the latter, it must mean *represents* in the former.[1]

---

[1] " Let those words," says Mr. Moule, " be fully preserved in our interpretation, and let the sacred Blood have its place of *distinct* and *equal* honour, and it will be seen that a very large range of inferences, sometimes taught as if directly revealed truths, prove to have no

Every Bible student is familiar with this use. It demands no cloud of explanatory words. The two sentences now stand in obvious self-interpreting simplicity. Are you perplexed when the same Divine voice says to St. John, "The seven candlesticks which thou sawest are the seven churches;" or when St. Paul writes, "This Agar is Mount Sinai in Arabia"? It is a use familiar still. "What is that banknote?" "It is £50;" and not a single additional word is needed to explain.

It is interesting to recall the fact that words somewhat similar to our Lord's were, and are still, common at the Passover feast. When the Jew next keeps the feast with his family, he will take in his hand the unleavened cake, and say, "This is the bread of affliction which our fathers did eat in the land of Egypt." That ancient formula was familiar, say some good authorities, to the little group of simple-hearted men who gathered round their Master at the Passover He had so eagerly desired; and, as He took the bread in the ha ids so soon to be pierced for them, it may well have interpreted to them His meaning. They could not in any case misunderstand Him. The New Covenant in His Blood was to have its sacred seals and symbols as well as the Old, which now passed away. "This is My Body which is

basis in the words of our Lord Himself. His words point directly, not to glory, but to death; not to the throne, but to the Cross; to Propitiation, Atonement, Sacrifice, Offering—there completed for ever" ("Outlines of Christian Doctrine," p. 262).

given for you ; " " This cup is the New Covenant in My Blood which is shed for you." Blessed Master, I, too, cannot mistake Thee. This bread broken, this wine out-poured, are lively images to my heart of Thy Body given, and Thy Blood shed, for me ; and, as oft as I eat this bread and drink this cup, I do it in remembrance of Thee.

Too many Christians stop here. They forget that there is more than this, for St. Paul says : " The cup of blessing which we bless, is it not a communion of the Blood of Christ ? The bread which we break, is it not a communion of the Body of Christ ? " (1 Cor. x. 16, R.V.) But here, too, the meaning is perfectly simple. There are two givers at this sacred feast—the minister, who gives to our senses the bread and wine, and the Holy Spirit, who gives to our faith the Body and Blood of Christ. The believer receives both, and both simultaneously ; the unbeliever, who comes without faith, receives only one. Well does Hooker say : " The real presence of Christ's most blessed Body and Blood is not to be sought for in the Sacrament, but in the worthy receiver of the Sacrament." Do you ask what it is to receive His Body and His Blood ? Surely it is once again as sinners to grasp the seal of the Covenant—the visible pledge of His finished atonement ; it is once again to identify ourselves with the Crucified, who, in His great love, identified Himself with us. It is more ; it is for our souls to feed upon Him by faith—it is *by this effectual means* to receive Himself. Language fails here. Suffice it to know that by all the grace this sacrament can convey, we are one with Him, and He with us. And yet, let us beware of mere sentiment and emotion even here. I am dealing to-night with essential doctrine, the safeguard of all devotional feeling, and I would have you listen to the great Waterland. He is writing in 1737 on the words of the Catechism : "The Body and Blood of Christ are verily and indeed taken and received by the faithful in the Lord's Supper ;" and he says, "The Body and Blood of Christ are taken and received by the faithful not corporeally, not internally, but verily and indeed—that is, *effectually.* The sacred symbols are no mere signs, as untrue figures of a thing absent, but the force, the grace, and the virtue of Christ's Body broken and Blood shed — that is, of His Passion—are really and effectually present with all them that receive worthily. This is all the real presence that our Church teaches." [1]

[1] It is evident, I think, that Waterland had in his mind Cranmer's words. Remembering how large a share the Archbishop had both in the Reformation and in the construction of our Articles, these words become especially important. "When I say, and repeat many times in my book, that the Body of Christ is present in them that worthily receive the Sacraments, lest any man should mistake my words, and think I mean that, though Christ be not corporally in the outward visible signs, yet He is corporally in the persons that duly receive them : this is to advertise the reader I mean no such thing ; but my meaning is that *the Force, the Grace, the Virtue,* and *Benefit* of Christ's Body that was crucified

I might multiply such quotations from the makers of the Prayer-Book. I might quote Ridley, Hooper, and other fathers of the English Church, but I forbear—I will only refer you to Dean Goode's *Presence of Christ in the Eucharist*—a monumental work that has never yet been answered.

It is in exact accordance with all this that our Church speaks again and again. "Hear the Church!" is a common cry in some pulpits. Well, they that have ears to hear, let them hear. Article XXVIII. says thus : "The Body of Christ is given, taken, and eaten in the Supper, only after an heavenly and spiritual manner. And the mean whereby the Body of Christ is received and eaten in the Supper is faith." Hear the Church ! Article XXIX. says thus : "The wicked, and such as be void of a lively faith, although they do carnally and visibly press with their teeth (as Saint Augustine saith) the Sacrament of the Body and Blood of Christ, yet in no wise are they partakers of Christ ; but rather to their condemnation do eat and

for us, and of His Blood that was shed for us, be really and effectually present with all them that duly receive the Sacraments. But all this I understand of His spiritual presence, of the which He saith, 'I will be with you until the world's end ;' and, 'Wheresoever two or three be gathered together in My name, there am I in the midst of them ;' and, 'He that eateth My Flesh and drinketh My Blood dwelleth in Me, and I in him.' Nor, no more truly, is He corporally or really present in the due ministration of the Lord's Supper than He is in the due administration of Baptism—that is to say, in both spiritually by grace " (Cranmer's Works on the Lord's Supper, Preface, Parker Society, Edit., 1884, p. 3).

drink the sign or sacrament of so great a thing "—words fatal to the High Church contention, for " the sign or sacrament " of a thing is unquestionably not the thing itself.

Hear the Church ! In the exhortation of her Prayer-Book to intending communicants she says, " The benefit is great if with a true penitent heart and lively faith we receive that Holy Sacrament, for then we spiritually eat the Flesh of Christ and drink His Blood." To such, and to such only, is this Sacrament an Effectual Sign. By *efficacia signa* Article XXV. means necessarily no more than " signs (seals) which do seal-work effectually." There is a vague but thoroughly baseless idea among many that it means signs which do effectually *something else*, supposed to be very mysterious. "They are *efficacia signa*," writes a well-known Cambridge scholar, " just as the wax on a deed duly ' delivered ' is *efficax* (*i.e.*, effectual), and that seems to me the gist of the word." But the Black Rubric at the end of the Communion Office makes it mere waste of time to add anything more as to the Prayer-Book view. I will only say, Hear the Church for yourselves, and, if words mean anything at all, the teaching that has leavened first Oxford, and then the Church of England, is not Church teaching at all.

No wonder that Hurrell Froude, with his Tractarian views, should speak of the Communion Service of the Church of his fathers as "a judgment" upon her ; or that Williams, in Tract 86, should represent the substitution of " table " for " altar " as a " judicial humiliation." The Oxford leaders, at any rate, saw what its language meant, and some of them honestly left our Communion.

I owe to Mr. Odom the following words of Dean Vaughan upon this vital subject, with which I will conclude. He says : " That it should be given to man, instrumentally by hand or tongue, to create God — to turn common bread, common wine, by a few movements of the hand and a few utterances of the lips, into the very Body and Blood of Him who made the worlds—this was the keystone of that arch of priestly domination which once bestrode the world. It was this that made possible the domestic tyranny of the confessional, it was this that drew the life-blood of our English martyrs, who felt that its overthrow was worth the dying for.

" It is this which English innovators, calling themselves restorers, would now bring back upon us ; from whose errors, or follies, or impostures—call them what you will—may God evermore preserve His true, His faithful, His Apostolical Church of England." To all which I say, with all my heart, Amen.

The Book of Common Prayer.

"Prove all things ; hold fast that which is good."
I THESSALONIANS V. 21.

THE Book of Common Prayer is the priceless possession of all Englishmen, and especially of all English Churchmen. Next to the English Bible, that other trophy of the Reformation, it has influenced for three centuries the English language, the standard of Faith, the devotion of our race. Wherever the English language is spoken—and even beyond that limit—our Prayer-Book is known and held in just esteem.

The Prayer-Book was not, however, a new book at the Reformation : it was a republication or modification of the different Uses or Services, such as those of Sarum, York, Bangor, Hereford, and others, which had slowly grown up during the centuries, and which were themselves the development of still earlier liturgies. In fact, as Dean Burgon says, the Prayer - Book "exhibits the accumulated wisdom, not of a single age or country, but of all the ages. The East has contributed her purest traditions ; the West has enshrined them in a casket of her wisest contriving ; and piety has gathered up the gems of the holiest utterance wherever syllabled, careful only to conceal the blessed speaker's name. In all its essential outlines, it has been the consolation of God's people—of our fathers, and of our fathers' fathers—for more than a thousand years." The Prayer-Book is essentially a devotional handbook for true believers ; it speaks, as you will recollect, to all as Christians. That it could not do otherwise I explained fully in speaking on Baptism.

I. To-night, I wish to draw your attention to some of the inestimable advantages that our Liturgy secures to us, and then to close with a few words on what I conceive to be the present position and duty of Evangelical Churchmen.

Never, I suppose, was it of more importance to have a clear understanding of both the letter and spirit of our Prayer-Book, and of the history of its compilation. He who is well informed on these points will be secured, by God's grace, from Popish error on one side, and Puritan innovation on the other.

The first thing, then, I want to emphasise is this, that in our Liturgy we have a Guarantee of Orthodoxy. This is no small advantage, as history teaches us. Those who have studied the development of the Churches tell us that even Calvin's scriptural doctrine in course of time, not only in Geneva, but in many of the Presbyterian congregations in England, Ireland, and the United States, gradually and silently gave way to a bare Socinianism.[1] So long as our Prayer-Book remains, it cannot

[1] See Fausset, p. 8.

be so with ourselves. We cannot *utterly* fall away. In our churches, the pulpit here and there may be worse than useless ; "dead preachers may speak to dead sinners the living truths of the living God." It may be infected with the down-grade theology of the time—the children may cry for bread and get a stone ; or, it may be semi-popish, and inculcate the Real Presence, and adoration of the elements ; but always the error of the pulpit's teaching will to some extent be corrected by that of the desk ; for our Prayer-Book, as its preface indicates, has this as its chief feature—its adherence to the Word of God. Take away the Bible out of the Prayer-Book, and how little you have left ! I believe that no other Liturgy in the world is quite equal to our own in this. Not merely is scripture publicly read, and congregationally sung, in every part of our public worship ; but the responses, collects, ascriptions and special offices are simply steeped in Bible thought and Bible language. No man, it is not too much to say, can enter our churches and use *intelligently* our incomparable Liturgy without learning his need as a sinner, the way of salvation, and the outline of Christian life. Yes, the very warp and woof of our Prayer-Book is the Word of God, and this is chiefly what gives it its inestimable value.

Again, let me remind you of the advantage of our Liturgical forms in securing hearty Congregational Worship. No one can doubt the lawfulness of such forms, since our Lord taught us how to pray ; but do we Church-men sufficiently appreciate the gain ? Does any Church give to the congregation so large a share in its services as our own ? We have emphatically a book of Common—that is of joint—Prayer. In the first century, a heathen thus describes a Christian Liturgy—"The worshippers repeat a formula to Christ as God, in alternate responses." Could any description be more happy of parts of our own ? Greatly as I value extempore prayers in our weekly prayer-meeting, how much should we not lose if we were thus limited in our public worship ! We all know what we are going to pray for. We agree on earth as touching certain matters. We pray *with* the minister, not immediately after him. We have not to guess what he is going to say, nor are we anxious as to whether his doctrine or political views will make it difficult for us to say heartily, *Amen.*

Once I was told that a good Christian man declared he could not attend our worship, because there were four or five things he could not agree to in the Liturgy. I sent him a message that if that were so, he ought to join us forthwith, for in Church he knew exactly beforehand all that he could take exception to ; in chapel, he could never be sure, and only hope for the best ! It was a new light, and he came henceforth. How dear these familiar words are, and familiarity is a help, not a hindrance, to devotion. We have not even to think of them, but simply of the wants which they so admirably unfold, and of Him to Whom we come.[1] "If a sensible person," says Charles Simeon, "were to write down *all* the prayers that were uttered under the name of extempore prayer, in different chapels, for one Sunday, he would fall down on his knees, and thank God for the Liturgy of the Church of England."

It is this ancient Liturgy which links together devout Churchmen all the world over, and, year by year, carries them through the whole cycle of Christian doctrine. I like, too, to think of it as one special bond of union between ourselves and those who go forth from us to the Mission field. One of our number has just reached her destination on the shores of the Niger ; another sailed last week for Northern India ; yet another will be dismissed this week for Japan : but week by week we shall all use the same words at the same Throne of Grace wherever we are. Surely, if it is a sacred delight to realise in our

[1] Canon Fausset tells of a Durham pitman that, being found reading the Litany, he was asked why he loved the Prayer-Book. He answered, "One sentence in this book, if there were no other, would of itself be sufficient to save the world. It is this : 'O holy, blessed, and glorious Trinity, three Persons and one God, have mercy upon us miserable sinners.' Oh! sir, what have I experienced in these words! I have felt the sweet drawings of a Father's love, the cleansing power of a Saviour's blood, and the sanctifying influences of the Holy Spirit's grace ; and I have felt my whole soul entwined, as it were, in the sacred Three." Some Christians object to call themselves "miserable sinners," or to confess that "the burden of their sins is intolerable." I admit that we need to walk very close with God to use these words honestly.

Communion Service that we unite in praise with angels and archangels, and with all the company of heaven, in the very words of their Tersanctus ; it is only a lesser delight to know that in these prayers, hallowed by a thousand years, we unite with saints in every part of the world below.

Once again, have you ever thought how thoroughly Protestant our Liturgy is ? Some of you have been perplexed, doubtless, by a sentence here and there which seems to be otherwise, and instead of interpreting such sentences by the Prayer-Book as a whole, you have just reversed the process, and judged the Prayer-Book by those sentences. Nothing more suicidal could be well conceived, under present circumstances, than to put a Romish interpretation upon passages which we know were never so meant by the compilers. Nothing can damage our Protestant Church more. It is well to remember that when, in Elizabeth's reign, the Pope licensed concealed Jesuits who should feign themselves Churchmen for the purpose of sowing the seeds of disaffection in the Church of England, one of their chief instruments was the topic that the Prayer-Book had not been sufficiently reformed.[1] Of course, the Prayer-Book could be amended—there is but one book that could not ; but do remember that our Liturgy as it stands is a standing witness against Popery. " Away with the

[1] On this whole subject see the late learned Dean Goode's remarkable little book, " Rome's Tactics," published for threepence by Nisbet.

old rubbishy opinion," says the Bishop of Liverpool, "that the Church of England occupies a middle position, a *via media*, between Dissent and Rome. You might as well talk of the Isle of Wight being midway between England and France. Between us and Rome there is a gulf both broad and deep ; between us and orthodox Protestant Dissent there is but a partition wall. Between us and Rome the division is in essentials ; between us and Dissent the division is about things in which a man may err and be saved." In like manner you will remember that while our Church speaks in clear and tolerant tones as to other orthodox Protestant communities, she declares the central act of worship of the Latin Church to consist of " blasphemous fables and dangerous deceits."

No ; if you want to know the real teaching of our Church, do not take, I pray you, an isolated sentence here and there out of the devotional parts of her Liturgy, but study her own authoritative declaration of her doctrines. Ask the Lutheran or Presbyterian the teaching of his church, and he will at once refer you to the Confessions of Augsburg or Westminster. Ask the Churchman, and he too often forgets the Thirty-nine Articles. These Articles were, to a large extent, the outcome of the Romish Council of Trent, and were formulated as an emphatic protest against its decrees ; for although that Council, which began in 1545, did not conclude until 1564, and our Articles were issued in 1562, yet the leading dogmas of the Tridentine fathers were in the hands of our Reformers long before the latter date. It was in opposition to them that Archbishop Cranmer with Ridley drew up forty-two articles, which, after a subsequent revision by Archbishop Parker, Grindal, and Cox, were reduced to thirty-nine, and were solemnly agreed upon by the whole body of bishops and clergy gathered in London under Queen Elizabeth.

Bishop Christopher Wordsworth thus writes :—

"The Thirty-nine Articles of Religion contain an exposition of the doctrines of the Church of England. They contain no enactment of anything new in doctrine, but they are only a declaration of what is old. In them the Church of England affirms that Holy Scripture containeth all things necessary to salvation."

God forbid that I should say anything calculated to stir up strife, but when I read in the *Church Times* that Lord Halifax, the President of the English Church Union, said at their annual meeting, at the close of a carefully weighed speech, "We must strive for Union, especially with the great Latin Church, from which we were separated by the sins of the sixteenth century," and when I remember that by the "sins of the sixteenth century" he means the Reformation, and when I remember further that there can be no union with Rome except on the terms of absolute submission—a submission involving, as Dr. Salmon says, "an acknowledgment that we from our hearts believe things to be true which we have good reason for knowing to be false "—then I say unhesitatingly that, however devout and earnest and self-sacrificing many of its members undoubtedly are, the English Church Union is simply a dissenting body within our fold, in which *loyal* Churchmen can find no place.[1]

You all know how advanced a Churchman the late Bishop Wilberforce of Winchester was. I ask you to hear some of his last words, addressed in 1873 to his Rural Deans. "There is a growing desire," he says, "to introduce novelties, such as incense, a multitude of lights in the chancel, and so on. Now these and such things are *honestly and truly alien to the Church of England.* Do not hesitate to treat them as such. There is a growing feeling which I can only describe as an ashamedness of the Anglican Church ; as if our grand old Anglican Communion contrasted unfavourably with the Church of Rome. The habitual language held by many men sounds as if they were *ashamed* of our Church and its position ; it is a sort of apology for the Church of England as compared with the Church of Rome. Why, I would as soon think of apologising for the virtue of my mother. I have no sympathy in the world with such a feeling. I abhor this fidgety desire to make everything un-Anglican. It is not a grand development,

---

[1] See Bishop Ryle's, "What is Written about the Lord's Supper" (Hunt), and Archdeacon Farrar's "Sacerdotalism" (National Protestant Church Union)—pamphlets that should be widely known.

as some seem to think — it is a decrepitude. It is not something very sublime and impressive, but something very feeble and contemptible." What would the Bishop say if he saw the length things have gone to *now ?*

II. In the second place, I want to say a few words about our present position as Evangelical Churchmen, and our consequent duty. For many years past an appeal has been made from time to time to courts of law, under well-known Acts of Parliament, as to certain ritualistic practices in different churches, and one by one these, or most of them, have been pronounced illegal. The Church Association, or any other body of Churchmen, was perfectly entitled to ascertain the law, which was admittedly obscure, and this it has done. Where, I venture to think, that Association made a mistake was in further proceeding to enforce the law when it was openly set at defiance. It was a mistake from the New Testament point of view ; it was a mistake in policy also. The spectacle of a clergyman in prison, "just because of his Church views," as people thoughtlessly said, awoke sympathy in tens of thousands entirely ignorant upon the real question involved. The bishops, who ought to have acted at first, shirked their responsibility until it was too late. I do not altogether blame them ; their power is but small. A bishop told me it had cost him personally £400 to oust an unworthy clergyman from his benefice. Doubtless the law needs amending ; but Convocation, if it had the will, certainly has not the power ; and

Parliament, which never will concede the power, certainly has not the will. The final result of this appeal to law has been, as you know, the Lincoln Judgment. The highest Ecclesiastical Court has confirmed the judgment of the Archbishop's Court, and has reversed all previous decisions. It has said that practices, which Bishop Wilberforce declared alien to the Church of England, are not illegal in the administration of the Lord's Supper. It is useless to complain. The appeal was to Cæsar, and Cæsar has spoken. I feel, therefore, it is important to remind you of two things. First, that the utmost declared by the judgment about any of these things is that they are *not illegal.* Secondly, that both courts declare that these practices, though permitted, are *not to be taken as having any doctrinal signification.* The position of Evangelical Churchmen, therefore, is not affected in the slightest. To talk of leaving the Church of our fathers is the language of irritation, and not of reason. The judgment shakes our confidence in courts of law—it does not alter our position as Churchmen ; we are exactly where we were. For this we may thank God and take courage.

What, in conclusion, is our duty ? Two-fold, I take it, in the main. First, hear the apostle speak : " If it be possible, as much as lieth in you, live peaceably with all men." We have the Prayer-Book and the Articles. We have the earliest Fathers ; we have all the great Divines of the Church of England down to fifty years ago ; we have the lessons of history, all on our side. We may well be satisfied. I am a strong Churchman. I know why I am not a Roman Catholic, and I know why I am not a Nonconformist. I also know why I am an Evangelical Churchman, and I am prepared, humbly by the grace of God, to maintain my position. Of one thing I am sure, it is possible to contend earnestly for the faith once delivered to the saints without breaking the ever-new Commandment of Love. If we cannot, depend upon it our position is not worth the fighting for. The matters at stake in this controversy are too tremendous for loss of temper. They are not mere questions of music, or banners, or of a trifling ceremonial ; they are questions of God's truth and of Man's salvation. Contention there must be ; but, I repeat, it must be in the spirit of love, or it will be contention in vain ; and I say that every Evangelical Churchman ought, above all things, to know why he is what he is. "Prove all things ; hold fast that which is good."

Secondly, Adorn the doctrine you profess. If Evangelical Churchmanship means anything, it means not merely the head clear, but the heart right with God. It means a personal knowledge of Christ as a personal Saviour, and of the sanctifying power of the Holy Spirit. It means an intelligent love of the Bible ; a growing unworldliness ; an openly avowed love to all who love our Lord in sincerity and truth, be they Churchmen or Nonconformists ; an ever intenser desire for the salvation of souls at home and abroad. In a word, it means that practical spirituality of life which is at once our only real power, and our justification before men. Any weapons but those of the Spirit will break in our hands and wound us. Use *these*, and as Christians we shall glorify God, and as Churchmen we shall be a blessing to our country.

I feel that I might speak to you upon the importance of Organisation, of a clearer manifestation to the world of the actual Unity that exists among us, but these things would be beyond my scope to-night. Words of inspiration run in my mind ; hear them as I close : " By pureness, by knowledge, by long-suffering, by kindness, by the Holy Ghost, by love unfeigned, by the word of truth, by the power of God, by the armour of righteousness on the right hand and on the left, by honour and dishonour, by evil report and good report : as deceivers, and yet true ; as unknown, and yet well known ; as dying, and behold we live ; as chastened, and not killed ; as sorrowful, yet alway rejoicing; as poor, yet making many rich ; as having nothing, and yet possessing all things " (2 Cor. vi. 6–10).

The Relative Importance of the different Means of Grace.

" And this I pray, that your love may abound yet more and more in knowledge and in all judgment ; that ye may approve things that are excellent ; that ye may be sincere and without offence till the day of Christ."—PHIL. i. 9, 10.

"THAT ye may approve the things that are excellent" ; that is, in the original Greek, "That between things that are alike excellent you may judge or distinguish "—exactly bringing us to our subject to-night, " The relative importance of the different means of grace."

We all feel that we live in perplexing times. In the State there is admittedly an upheaval, and on all sides we see indications of social and political convulsion. In the Churches, amid many activities, we have distinct evidence in some directions of decadence. There is a marked decay of the Lord's Day observance. There is a conformity to the world. There is a growing use of worldly means for spiritual ends ; and now and again the papers tell us of some terrible divorce, in church or chapel, of the gospel and common honesty, which it is painful, but necessary, to confess.

Why do I mention these things ? Because I believe them to be closely connected with

our subject. I believe that on observing the
relative importance of the means of grace
depends to a considerable extent the spiritual
life of the individual Christian. I believe that
Churchmen especially, with their authorised
standards of faith and doctrine, and holding
the position they do, have a grave responsibility in this matter ; and that, when a majority
of them ignorantly invert these divinely
ordered proportions, we may reasonably expect
a decay of spiritual life in the Church, which
will be quickly reflected in the nation at large,
and in the tone of the House of Commons.

That such an inversion has taken place I
shall attempt to show. Surely the question
is one of the highest importance, for, what are
the means of grace?   What, indeed, is grace?
Simply this—God in action towards sinful men
in Christ Jesus ; and by " means of grace " we
understand those ordained channels in and
through which He is usually pleased to act.
As I utter the words, my heart goes up in
wonder at the multitudinous means God has
provided. It is as if He, Who from the beginning " rejoiced in the habitable parts of the
earth," longed to use every means, that even
Divine Wisdom could devise, of intercourse
and communion with His creatures. And yet,
just as the colours of the rainbow, blending in
one harmonious whole, are nevertheless distinct, and bear a definite relation the one to
the other, on which the perfection of the whole
depends, so is it with the different means of
grace. I can of course only select. I will take
four of the most important, upon some of

which I have already spoken, viz., the Christian Ministry, the Sacraments, the Scriptures, and Prayer. With all the fairness I can, I shall endeavour to show the relative importance attached to these by the dominant party in our Church, and then state what I believe that proportion is designed by God to be.

I. There can be no question but that in the minds of a majority of our most zealous Church-people the ordained Ministry occupies a position that it has not occupied for three hundred years. The theory of apostolical succession is widely held in its most naked form— that the Bishops are the representatives of the Apostles, and the heirs of their spiritual power ; and this by virtue of a direct devolution of that power through an unbroken succession of laying on of hands, down from the Apostolic age itself. The logical issue of this view is found in the common formula, " No Bishop, no Church." To the second order of the Ministry are widely assigned sacerdotal titles, functions, and powers ; "on which," to use Mr. Gore's words, "the validity of the Sacraments depends." There is an increasing number who believe that by virtue of the Priest's *Absolvo te*, heard in the Confessional, all sin is remitted ; [1] and a multitude, who do not go so far as this, do heartily believe that certain words of consecration change, if not

[1] A few years ago the Confessional was rare, now it is habitually used in 177 churches in London alone, and is being introduced everywhere. In some churches, I am told, it is even made a *condition* of receiving the Lord's Supper.

7

the visible substance of the bread and wine, at least their essential character.   While refusing the Roman doctrine of Transubstantiation, their own formula as to the presence of Christ in the sacred elements differs from it in words only ; while as to the offering of Christ in the Eucharistic Sacrifice, there is not even a verbal difference.   The result is what we see.   The Holy Communion is pushed into the very first place among the means of grace.   It is the grand remedy for the spiritual needs of all the baptized.   "Come to the Holy Altar as par-takers, and, if not, as worshippers," is the call from hundreds of our pulpits week by week.[1] Again and again we are told that it is the chief act of worship, as well as the chief means of holiness.   Everything is sacrificed (I speak advisedly) to the sacrifice of the Altar.   It is not long since a leading High Church organ condoned the spending of the Lord's Day in pleasure, if only the Supper, instituted in the evening, were taken first thing in the morning. Evening Communion is an abomination be-cause it cannot be received, as it is said it should be, fasting.   In short, as "No Bishop, no Church," so it is distinctly held, "No Priest, no sacrament."

Just as clearly as the Sacraments have been exalted among the means of grace, so the Bible has taken a lower place in the hearts of myriads of honest Churchmen.   About this there can be no question ; indeed it is openly avowed

[1] "The Sacraments were not ordained of Christ to be gazed upon, or to be carried about, but that we should duly use them " (Article XXV.).

that the Bible, and the Bible only, is the secret of an uncatholic Protestantism. " The Bible and tradition, the Bible and primitive an tiquity, the Bible and the voice of the early Church, contain together the rule of faith." Ever since Keble published Tract 78, and declared that Scripture and Tradition together are the joint Rule of Faith, this doctrine has been proclaimed upon the housetops. This fully accounts, I maintain, for the lower esteem in which the Bible is held by the mass of the Ritualistic party. The Scriptures, we are told, are not to be put hastily into the hands of the young and ignorant ; and I can speak confidently as an old Oxford man, who has kept touch, so far as he may, with the Oxford Movement, that a large proportion of zealous Anglicans practically do not read their Bibles at all. Nor can I wonder, when only the other day I heard a prominent Ritualistic clergyman laugh publicly at the idea that the Bible is "the Word of God." Do not mistake me ; I must not weaken my position by overstating it. What is true of many is certainly not true of all. The High Church party is rent in twain to-day upon this very question. Mr. Gore's unproved hypotheses about the Old Testament have been greedily welcomed by many, for the supposed claims of the Church are not consistent with the claims of the Bible. On the other hand, all honour to Archdeacon Denison, and those High Churchmen with him, who firmly uphold the Divine authorship and supremacy of Holy Writ.

The last of the means of grace I take up is Prayer. Thank God, prayer is insisted on by High Churchmen as well as ourselves. I am sure there are scores of devout men, from whom I totally differ on important Church matters, with whom I should count it a privilege to kneel in prayer ; but, speaking of the party as a whole, I think I may ask with affectionate anxiety — Does *private* prayer occupy the place it should ? Is there not a real danger of the supposed claims of public worship invading the sacred duties of the closet ? We have been plainly told by one of their journals that prayers said in the church are more acceptable to God than prayers said in the chamber ; and I say sadly I have reason to fear that numbers of well-meaning Churchmen are giving up, first, Family Prayer, that great bond of the Christian family, for Matins ; and then the sacred communion of the closet for the Early Celebration in the church. This will bear further fruit in the same direction. The effects of the loudly proclaimed theory of priestly intercession are visible already, and in scores of churches day by day the clergyman may be seen monotoning morning prayer to a congregation consisting of some of his own family and the verger. I greatly fear that the principle, " *Qui facit per alium facit per se,*" is leading to deserted closets and to frequent services, and frequent services tend too often to empty churches. I am most anxious not to exceed the limits of actual fact in what I am saying. I repeat that I am not alluding to individuals but to the

High Church party as a whole ; and I say that, so far as I can judge, the Ministry is held first in esteem among the means of grace ; because neither Church nor Sacraments, it is supposed, can exist without it ; and Scripture and Prayer take distinctly lower places. I believe this order to be an inverted order ; I believe it to be full of danger both to Church and State ; and I shall now proceed to indicate what I believe to be the true relative importance of these means of grace.

II. As loyal Churchmen, I claim that we yield to none in the value we set upon the Christian Ministry. We hold an ordained ministry to be a special gift of our ascended Lord. We accept the threefold order of Bishop, Priest, and Deacon. We claim emphatically the historical succession of the Church of England. Episcopacy we hold essential to the well-being, not to the being, of a church ; but we do *not* hold apostolical succession in the sense asserted as essential. We hold it to be a theory incapable of proof, and worth nothing spiritually if it were proved. Carefully guarding as we do Episcopal ordination, we cling to our Church Article, and will not for a moment allow that the last fledgling admitted to Holy Orders, be he good, bad, or indifferent, is a true minister of Jesus Christ ; and that Matthew Henry, and Doddridge, and Robert Hall, and Chalmers, and Spurgeon were nothing of the kind.

As to the second order of the Ministry, we deny emphatically that any Presbyter can do more than authoritatively declare the terms upon which God is pleased to forgive sins. As to the Sacraments, we would point out that, in regard to that of Baptism, its validity so little depends upon apostolic succession, that it does not necessarily depend upon a clergyman at all ; but may be administered under certain circumstances by a layman, or even by a midwife, and it cannot be repeated.

In the Lord's Supper we maintain jealously that the bread and wine are bread and wine still ; nothing more and nothing less. We assert, with our Article, that the blessing of the Sacrament—which is indeed nothing less than the communion of the Body and Blood of Christ—depends wholly and entirely upon the hearts of those who receive, and not upon the hands of those who consecrate ; and we hold that the adoration now so commonly offered to the Presence in the consecrated elements, is dangerously akin to "idolatry, to be abhorred of all faithful Christians." We deny altogether any sacerdotal character whatever to the Presbyter of the Church of England, save and except that which every Christian shares, whether he be cleric or lay. We say, with Hooker, that "Sacrifice is no part of our Church's ministry" ; and we appeal to antiquity, and say that the earliest Fathers never asserted it was.

Our position is perfectly clear, and confidently we claim Bible, Prayer-Book, and History, and the greatest Divines of the English Church, in support of it ; but if so, the Sacraments stand on a wholly different footing from that commonly assigned · to them, and we must discover some other principle for determining their relative importance.

III. I venture to lay down three propositions. First, that the proportionate value of any doctrine, or ordinance of the Christian Faith, must be ascertained by the frequency and urgency with which it is enforced in the Bible, and especially in the Epistles ; which teach doctrines, just as the Gospels mainly record the facts on which those doctrines are based. Apply this test to the Lord's Supper ; and, if accustomed to the extravagant language of the day, you will be positively startled by the contrast, and by the small place it relatively occupies in the New Testament.

About Faith and Works, about Holiness and Unholiness, about Justification and Sanctification, we have line upon line, and precept upon precept. About the Lord's Supper, you will find that blessed ordinance is mentioned in one single Epistle, and that in all the other twenty it is not so much as mentioned. The Bishop of Liverpool (Dr. Ryle) says : " In the Pastoral Epistles to Timothy and Titus, where one might certainly expect to find detailed instructions about the Lord's Supper, it is conspicuously absent. Now I cannot get over that fact. The silence of Scripture is just as eloquent as its voice." This argument of course is flouted, but I have not yet seen it answered. It seems to me a perfectly obvious contention ; and in using it I am glad to find an ally, unconscious of course, in Mr. Sadler, in his " Church Doc-

trine, Bible Truth." "Judged by their
respective services," he says (p. 117), "Baptism has a far higher position in the English
than in the Romish Church." And he proves
it thus, "In the Romish office the administration of the Sacrament itself is thrust into a
corner, and four-fifths of the Service have
to do with other ceremonies (exorcisms,
benedictions, and the like), so that in a copy
of the 'Rituale Romanum' now before me,
out of ten pages occupied by the Baptismal
Service, not two have to do with the Sacrament itself." Mr. Sadler's point is conclusive ;
but this is exactly our own argument from the
place the Lord's Supper holds in the New
Testament. If the inspired writers of the
first century were right in the way they dealt
with the Lord's Supper, I cannot help feeling
that some of the uninspired writers of the
nineteenth century are entirely wrong.

My second proposition is this : That the
relative importance of the means of grace may
be further ascertained by the admitted necessities of the regenerated soul. As there is an
analogy, divinely taught, between physical
and spiritual birth ; so there is a likeness
between the intuitive longings of the infant
and of the new-born soul. As the one cannot
be satisfied without its mother's milk, so the
other is athirst for God's Word. "As new-
born babes," writes St. Peter, "desire the
sincere milk of the word, that ye may grow
thereby." Again and again, until I take it as
one of the best evidences of the Spirit's quickening work, have I heard men say, "The

Bible has become a new book to me." Nor is this all ; as men grow in grace, the " sincere milk " is exchanged for the "strong meat " of their full manhood in Christ, and it is the eminent saint who cries, "Thy words were found, and I did eat them, and thy word was unto me the joy and rejoicing of mine heart " (Jer. xv. 16). " I," said Luther, " did not learn my divinity at one only time, but was constrained to search deeper and deeper, to which my temptations brought me ; for no man without trials and temptations can attain to the true understanding of the Holy Scriptures."

Hear, again, Ridley, our blessed martyr-bishop, whom Cambridge trained, and Oxford, I am sorry to say, burned ; he is writing just before his fiery death, and thus says he : " In thy orchard, Pembroke Hall (the wals, buttes, and trees, if they could speak would beare me witnes), I learned without booke almost all Paule's Epistles, yea, and I weene all the Canonicall Epistles, save only the Apocalyps. Of which study, although in time a great part did depart from me, yet the sweete smell thereof I trust I shall carry with me into heaven ; for the profite thereof I thinke I have felt in all my lyfe-tyme ever after." " So shall it be with us also," comments Mr. Moule, "if we go and do likewise in our ' lyfe-tyme '—our period, not at present of martyrdom, but, God knoweth it, of need."

And if we look humbly at Him who " left us an example that we should follow His steps," were not the daily needs of His human soul met, not by Sacraments, but by

the Old Testament writings? By His con-
stant use of them, not less than by His
emphatic vindication of the authenticity and
inspiration of the Old Testament Canon, we
learn their relative place. With the Scripture
He resisted the Tempter in the wilderness ;
with the Scripture He opened His mouth and
taught the people ; with the Scripture He
confuted scribe and Sadducee : " Ye do err, not
knowing the Scriptures, nor the power of
God " ; with the Scripture on His lips He died ;
and when the glorious Easter dawned, and He
revealed Himself to shattered hopes and aspi-
rations, it was once again to appeal to the
written Word, for, " beginning at Moses and all
the prophets, He expounded unto them in all
the scriptures the things concerning Himself."

And if the Master's needs were thus (though
not thus exclusively) met, how must it be with
the disciple ? We are not left in doubt. In
John vi. our Lord declares Himself to be the
living Bread come down from heaven, of which
if a man eat he shall live for ever. Not un-
naturally perplexed, His hearers seek to know
His meaning, and He explains it thus, " The
words that I have spoken " (*i.e.*, those last
utterances of Mine) " are spirit and are life " ;
" that is," says Bishop Westcott, " belong
essentially to the region of eternal being, and
so are *capable of conveying that which they
essentially are.*" " Lord, to whom shall we
go ? Thou hast the words of eternal life,"
cry the disciples, and our hearts echo their
cry. And as life comes through Christ's
words, so " he that *keepeth* them " is solemnly

declared to have fellowship with Father, Son, and Holy Spirit (John xiv.). The Epistles enlarge upon this teaching. St. James bids us "receive with meekness the implanted word, which is able to save your souls" (i. 21). St. Peter says, "Ye were born again *through* (διὰ) the word of God" (1 Pet. i. 23). The last of the apostles writes, "I have written unto you, young men, because ye are strong, and the word of God abideth in you, and ye have overcome the evil one" (1 John ii. 14). How impossible is the Ritualist's practical limitation of "the means of grace" to the two Sacraments in the light of typical passages such as these! If Simon Magus, baptized but still unregenerate, was ever to become a child of God, what other method for him was there but to receive, under the Spirit's teaching, the life-giving word?

If you want to know how a Churchman, firmly holding Primitive and Catholic doctrine, loves the Lord's Supper, I would have you read Adolphe Monod's "Farewell"; or, better still, the writings of the great Fathers of the English Church. It is simply grievous to have to attempt to compare the relative place of two such essential means of grace, nor would it be necessary but for the unprimitive and uncatholic teaching so prevalent about the Sacraments. Uncatholic, I repeat, for if "Catholic" means, among other things, "*quod semper*," it includes the New Testament times and teaching.

Our Church insists upon this proportion, if not in words, at least in practice. Her Liturgy, as I have shown you, is steeped in Scripture. Her Sixth Article declares : " Holy Scripture *containeth* all things necessary to salvation, so that whatsoever is not read therein, nor may be proved thereby, is not to be required of any man that it should be observed as an article of the Faith, or be thought requisite to salvation." How different her attitude towards that blessed Sacrament she so jealously guards from Zwinglian half-truth, or Roman innovation : "There shall be no communion except four (or three at the least) communicate with the Priest." And again in the Rubric concerning small parishes, " There shall be no celebration of the Lord's Supper, except there be a convenient number to communicate with the Priest according to his discretion." I ask emphatically, how dare our Church thus restrict the opportunities of Holy Communion ; making them, in fact, contingent on the number of communicants, or the discretion of the Curate, if she holds it to be "the highest means of grace " ? The place she assigns to Scripture and this Sacrament in her public services is eloquent of her view ; and certainly it is not he who thoughtfully adopts it who deserves to be called an ill-taught or disloyal Churchman.

High as is the position thus given to Scripture, there is, judging by the universal instincts of the regenerate soul, one means of grace more important still ; I mean, of course, Prayer. Prayer is closely linked with Scripture. The promises of God are the basis of prayer. The encouragement to prayer is the bidding of God. The best words of prayer

are often the very words of God ; but, nevertheless, first in order of time and of importance
is Prayer. The inarticulate cry of the new-
born babe is the first joyful intimation to the
mother's heart that a man is born into the
world ; and, " Behold, he prayeth," is God's
own convincing illustration of His quickening
work. Of our duty to the Scriptures nothing
is said like this : " Pray without ceasing "
(1 Thess. v. 17), or, " Praying always with all
prayer and supplication in the spirit " (Eph.
vi. 18). Here, again, his Lord's example in
prayer — deliberate, sustained, ejaculatory,
public, private, secret prayer—is the Christian's assurance both of the need and place
of prayer. " Prayer is the Christian's vital
breath." It is so on earth ; it will be so, we
believe, in heaven. Dear as is the Lord's
Supper to every true disciple, it is but a
pledge of something dearer far, the personal
visible presence of His Lord ; in this sense it
speaks to him of a real absence, for it is only
" till He come." In due time it will surrender
its place and use ; for when we gaze, with St.
Thomas, on Him " who was wounded for our
transgressions," Sacraments will be needed no
more. So, too, the Books of the Old and New
Covenants will cease perhaps to speak to us
when we see no more through a glass darkly,
and " know even as also we are known." But
through Eternity, I take it, Prayer will ever
mingle with Praise, and with ever deepening
meaning we shall cry, "Teach me to do Thy
will, for Thou art my God."

My last proposition is this : That we can,

to some extent, test the relative importance
of the different means of grace *by the effects
they produce.* Upon this only a few words
before I close, but uttered with a deep convic-
tion that they are substantially true.

It is by results, results visible in life and
conduct, that the truth of doctrines must
ultimately be tested. Christianity itself, compared with other systems of faith, must stand
or fall by this test. Within the Christian
faith there are a variety of means of grace,
some more, and some less, essential. Com-
mensurate with the claims put forth for one
or other of these, results must be apparent, or
the claims themselves become open to sus-
picion. "With Truth all facts and realities
agree," says Aristotle. Put modern claims as
to the Sacraments to this simple test, and what
do we find? We have the means of judging.
Let us take one important section of our
population, distinguished by its wealth, its
general intelligence, and better cared for by
the High Church clergy, as Mackeson's *Guide*
proves, than any other equal number of such
persons in the world. I mean, of course, those
who live in the West-End of London. Large
numbers attend church. Large numbers,
larger than ever before, are communicants.
Urged, persuaded, entreated, they come to
Holy Communion,[1] especially to early cele-

[1] Now openly called " The Mass " in many churches.
"We already have the *name*, we shall soon have the
thing," said an exultant Ritualist not long ago. Nor
do I think his prophecy unjustified. Already there are
more than one thousand churches in England where the
mediæval eucharistic vestments, the symbol of the sacer-

brations. Many of them doubtless are most sincere Christians, but how does a large proportion of them afterwards "kill Sunday"? I could speak from personal knowledge; but it is less invidious and more important to hear what the Bishops say. In their recent utterance on the growing desecration of the Lord's Day they speak with no uncertain sound; they are dealing with London Society that goes to church; and they tell of picnics on the Thames, of tennis parties, of fashionable visiting, of late dinners. Many of the High Church clergy lament it too. They do their best to check an increasing evil; they speak of it, they preach of it; but what never seems to occur to them is that the habit of many of their communicants condemns their own Eucharistic theory. Grace is not given, after all, by a mere reception of the elements; something does depend, it would seem, upon the heart and motive of the communicant. I am far from saying that Bible-reading and prayer are charms either: they are only channels, and sometimes empty channels. Here, too, grace depends upon something more than its appointed conduit; but, I put it to you, were you to hear that these same fashionable multitudes that throng, first, the rails of our West-End churches, and then "Church Parade" in the Park, had suddenly become earnest in Bible study, earnest in secret Prayer, would you expect London Society to continue what

dotal doctrine, are worn. Already seven Bishops have worn the obsolete mitre, discarded at the Reformation as a symbol of what was corrupt and not primitive.

it is to-day? And if not, why not? Does not your answer prove that in your inmost heart you do not believe the Lord's Supper occupies the place commonly claimed for it among the means of grace, and that other means, not less ordained of God, need to be exalted?

How shall I close? With a word of earnest exhortation to you personally. It is so easy to sit in judgment upon others, and to forget our own personal responsibility. Our communions are large, I greatly desire to see them larger; I want to see more of you coming to the Lord's Table, but coming only on those conditions which Scripture and our Church alike so clearly and certainly lay down—"Let a man examine himself, and so let him eat of that bread and drink of that cup" (1 Cor. xi. 28). For this, self-judgment in the light of the written word, and confession in the closet, are essential. If further help is needed, our Church bids him have recourse to that other appointed means of grace, "some discreet and learned Minister of God's Word, that *by the ministry of God's holy Word* he may receive the benefit of absolution, together with ghostly counsel and advice." Thus linking together these means of grace, the Scriptures, Prayer, the Ministry, and the Sacraments, you will find that the Divine Giver Himself blesses you by each and all of them; you will distinguish between one and the other while you delight in each; and you will, as a result, "glorify God in your bodies which are His."

UNWIN BROTHERS, PRINTERS, CHILWORTH AND LONDON.

www.ingramcontent.com/pod-product-compliance
Lightning Source LLC
Chambersburg PA
CBHW032112010726
47493CB00008B/2557